MARCH SISTERS

ON LIFE, DEATH,
AND *LITTLE WOMEN*

MARCH
SISTERS

KATE BOLICK

JENNY ZHANG

CARMEN MARIA MACHADO

JANE SMILEY

LIBRARY OF AMERICA
Special Publication

MARCH SISTERS: ON LIFE, DEATH, AND *LITTLE WOMEN*
Volume compilation copyright © 2019 by Literary Classics
of the United States, Inc., New York, N.Y.
"Meg's Frock Shock," by Kate Bolick. Copyright © 2019 by Kate Bolick.
"Does Genius Burn, Jo?" by Jenny Zhang.
Copyright © 2019 by Jenny Zhang.
"A Dear and Nothing Else," by Carmen Maria Machado.
Copyright © 2019 by Carmen Maria Machado.
"I Am Your 'Prudent Amy'" by Jane Smiley.
Copyright © 2019 by Jane Smiley.
All rights reserved.
Published in the United States by Library of America.
Visit our website at www.loa.org.

Interior design & composition by Gopa & Ted2, Inc.
Interior and endpaper illustrations by Kimberly Glyder.

Distributed to the trade in the United States by
Penguin Random House Inc. and in Canada
by Penguin Random House Canada Ltd.

Library of Congress Control Number: 2019932263
ISBN 978-1-59853-628-7

1 3 5 7 9 10 8 6 4 2

Printed in the United States of America

CONTENTS

PREFACE

As JANE SMILEY notes in the pages of this book, we tend to think and speak of Louisa May Alcott's Meg, Jo, Beth, and Amy as if they were real. Readers have had an intense interest in the stories of the four March sisters from the beginning. After the publication of part one of *Little Women* in 1868 (part two followed in 1869), Alcott was inundated with letters, many of them addressed to Jo, demanding to know what happened to the four sisters. "Girls write to ask who the little women marry, as if that was the only end and aim of a woman's life," Alcott wrote in her diary. "I *won't* marry Jo to Laurie to please any one." Readers would continue to send fan letters to Alcott's publisher until at least 1933, forty-five years after her death. In the decades after the novel's release, "*Little Women* clubs" became common across the country, with members taking on the identities of the March sisters, just as Meg, Jo, Beth, and Amy took on the identities of the Pickwick Society members in the novel. More recently, *Little Women* has served as inspiration to screenwriters, directors, and actors in more than a dozen film and television adaptations. Ursula K. Le Guin, Patti Smith, Susan Sontag, and J. K. Rowling, among numerous others, have claimed *Little Women* as an influence. Many more future novelists and feminists will be emboldened by Jo's example, while others will continue to find encouragement in Meg's egalitarian marriage, Beth's self-sacrifice and love of family, and Amy's relentless pursuit of art and beauty.

Often first encountered in early adolescence, *Little Women* is one of those childhood favorites readers return to in later years, for its pleasures are many and changeable, and its life lessons about love, loss, patience, duty, hard work, and of course marriage are always worth hearing (especially if one has forgotten them). Rereading *Little Women* in adulthood, we may appreciate complexities previously undetected, or we may, with the shock of recognition, come to understand something about our own childhood—and hence about ourselves. But *Little Women* remains primarily a book for young readers, and for girls especially. Alcott was blunt about her aims in writing about four sisters growing up in a small New England town—she once famously (and perhaps dismissively) called her work "moral pap for the young." But to say that *Little Women* was written to both delight and instruct is only to say it is a book like George Eliot's *Middlemarch* (1871–72) or John Bunyan's spiritual allegory *The Pilgrim's Progress* (1678, 1684), whose salubrious example is often invoked by the March parents. It is the kind of book in which readers find themselves.

Alcott knew how good a book she had written. "It reads better than I expected," she confessed in her journal in 1868. "Not a bit sensational, but simple and true, for we really lived most of it, and if it succeeds that will be the reason of it." This biographical dimension of the novel has undoubtedly increased our interest in the Marches, even as it has obscured their real-life antecedents (the Orchard House museum advertises itself as the home in which Alcott "set" *Little Women*). Tomboyish Jo was based on Alcott herself, known as Lou or Louie in the family. Like her hot-tempered counterpart, Bronson and Abba Alcott's second daughter had a "mood pillow" and helped to support her family by writing thrillers. Unlike Jo, she would never marry. Meg was based on Alcott's older sister Anna, who like Meg worked as a teacher but did not enjoy it. Unlike Meg, Anna went on from childhood theatricals to become an actress, performing in an amateur theater in Walpole, New Hampshire, and meeting John Pratt, the original of John Brooke, when they performed together in Concord. She married Pratt in May 1860, and had two sons, Frederick and John. Beth was based on the third Alcott sister, Lizzie. Like Beth, she was the shyest sister, nicknamed "Little Tranquility." Lizzie loved to play the piano (she was given one by a wealthy benefactor), and left school at fifteen to stay home and help keep house. When in spring 1856 she and younger sister May both contracted scarlet fever, Lizzie never fully recovered. She died at age twenty-two. And Amy was based on May, who acknowledged as much in a letter she wrote to her friend Alfred Whitman (one of the sources for Laurie) after the book was published: "Did you recognize . . . that horrid stupid Amy as something like me even to putting a cloths pin on her nose? . . . I used to be so ambitious, & think wealth brought everything." Like Amy, May was the pet of the family and longed to become a famous artist; a family friend paid her way to study in Boston with William Morris Hunt.

She was able to study in Europe only after the success of *Little Women* allowed Louisa to send her. During May's lifetime, her work was exhibited twice at the Paris Salon.

Four self-described fans of *Little Women*—Kate Bolick, Jenny Zhang, Carmen Maria Machado, and Jane Smiley—talk in this book about their personal connection to the novel and what it has meant to them (as children, adults, or both). More particularly, each of the writers takes in turn one of the March sisters as her subject. Kate Bolick finds parallels in the chapter about Meg attending the Moffats' ball to her own relationship—or resonance—with clothes. Jenny Zhang, when she first read *Little Women* as a girl, liked Jo least of the March sisters because Jo reflected Zhang's own quest for genius, which she feared was too unfeminine. Carmen Maria Machado writes about the real-life tragedy of Lizzie Alcott, and the horror story that can result from not being the author of your own life's narrative. And Jane Smiley rehabilitates the reputation of Amy, whom she sees as a modern feminist role model for those of us who are, well, not like the fiery Jo. Taken together, these pieces are a testament to the ways in which *Little Women*, like all great books, can become so entwined in our own life narratives that we must ask ourselves whether, had we never read it, we would be fully mindful of how we have lived—or even quite fully ourselves. May these four writers inspire you to reread *Little Women*—or perhaps to pick it up for the first time.

MARCH SISTERS

KATE BOLICK ON MEG

MEG'S FROCK SHOCK

"*LITTLE WOMEN* was about the best book I ever read." So began my fourth-grade book report, in 1981. Clear, if uninspired. After one-and-a-half double-spaced pages of cursive rhapsodizing in support of this daring claim, I concluded with the lazy feint of an already overburdened critic: "I would like to go on and on with this report but it would be longer than the book, so if you want to find the rest out my opinion is to read it."

I hadn't remembered this foray into criticism when I rediscovered it recently, at the bottom of an old wooden box in my childhood home. What I had remembered was the report's cover art—I'd never been more proud of anything I'd made—and my mother's irritation that I'd spent more time drawing it than I did writing about the book. Gingerly, I lifted the papers from the box and carried them to the sofa, astonished that thirty-seven years later this humble homework assignment still existed, curious to see what I'd been so worked up about.

Before I go on, I should note that though I'd loved *Little Women* as a child, I never thought about it as an adult. I cringe to admit how thoroughly I'd absorbed our culture's hypocrisy toward motherhood, but for most of my life I regarded Louisa May Alcott as matronly, and therefore dull. This flagrant misconception was based entirely on the world I'd found in that book, which was so snugly familiar, both physically and emotionally, that I simply took it for granted, the way I did my own mother. Our small town on the North Shore of Massachusetts in the late 1900s—especially during a snowstorm—didn't seem that different from Alcott's 1800s Concord, only forty-five miles south. Even the March family's puritanical streak ran through my own.

As I neared, my opinion changed. I was living alone in Brooklyn, working as a freelance writer, when I learned that in her thirties Alcott had lived on her own in Boston, doing the same thing. She never married or had children. She considered the social roles of "wife" and "husband" grievously prescriptive, and marriage akin to slavery, so long as women were kept economically and politically inferior to men. In February 1868, several months before she moved back home to help her parents, and started *Little Women*, she wrote an essay in praise of the single life, called "Happy Women." As she noted in her diary, on Valentine's Day no less, she had written it to celebrate "all the busy, useful, independent spinsters I know, for liberty is a better husband than love to many of us."

Celebrating independent spinsters was exactly what I'd been working to do at the time, in my first book. Upon further digging, I learned that Alcott didn't always feel so sanguine about her status; she was a passionate person, with strong maternal feeling, and up until her death regretted that the conventions of her era required women to sacrifice sex and motherhood if they also wanted to work. To know that she, too, grappled with the competing desires for autonomy and intimacy fascinated me, and I decided to return to *Little Women* to see how this ambivalent spinster had treated Meg's marriage. Even so, I allowed several more years to pass before I actually made time for it, little knowing how much more was in store.

As when I was nine, I couldn't put the book down.

Sinking into the story, I recalled the experience of being new to reading, the capacity to completely surrender myself to fiction. I saw, too, how this particular book had marked a departure from that habit of heedless abandon, when a mental image I'd long puzzled over arose: my nine-year-old self posing on the front stoop of our house, bare feet drawn up before me, *Little Women* open on my knees. When my friends arrived, they would find me like this, apparently so absorbed in my reading that I wouldn't hear their approach. So I had fantasized many times, anyway, I now realized.

Before *Little Women*, reading was just something I did, constantly and everywhere, at breakfast, during recess, stretched out in the backyard after school, by the fire with my parents, in bed before sleep. After reading about the March sisters' own reading, and about how much reading meant to them, I decided that reading was a romantic act, something to be proud of—even displayed. I'd had no idea Alcott played such an active role in the shaping of my self-identity. What else had I been missing?

What luck: that old book report cover contained a clue.

With colored pencils, I'd carefully drawn a giant oval

and put the March family inside it, like a miniature tab-
leau inside a sugar Easter egg. At center in a high-backed
green armchair is Jo, wearing a long lavender dress, slip-
pered feet drawn up before her, book open on her knees,
gazing straight at the viewer. Her parents stand behind
the chair—authoritatively, protectively—and on the
wall behind them hangs a framed portrait of Laurie, in
profile. The other sisters are all in profile as well: Beth
and Amy on the floor to Jo's left, with their customary
paraphernalia—one with needle and thread, the other
with pad and paintbrush—and to her right, Meg in a
rocking chair, embroidering, red dress bright as a Bald-
win apple, long curls so lustrous they tumble out of the
cameo frame. The depiction is as faithful to the novel as
my report had been.

The closer I looked, however, the more I saw. Jo is the
obvious protagonist of this portrait, and Meg a tantaliz-
ing lure. Even more intriguing, I'd taken creative license
with the details: though Jo is famously indifferent to
clothing, hers is the only dress that's embellished with a
hem of delicate pink roses, and poufed up, princess-style,
with not one but *two* frilly lace underskirts. In comparison, Meg's flat, unadorned frock is a nun's habit.

I suddenly remembered how, after the first time I

read *Little Women*, I began drawing pictures of girls in nineteenth-century fashions—hoop skirts and petticoats, aprons and cloaks, little lace-up boots with their intricate hooks and eyes. Constantly. It was a curious pastime for me. I had never been a girly-girl. The word "tomboy" fits, but imperfectly; it's not that I wanted to be a boy, or do only boyish things, but rather that my liberal-minded parents allowed me to inhabit a genderless space, and I looked the part. That summer, on my ninth birthday, in his consciously unsentimental "family diary," my father described me as being "of average height, slim but not skinny. Long, light brown hair, sort of lank, which is usually messy, and tends to need washing. For some reason she resists taking baths. Horrible teeth." School photos show I didn't yet know to be embarrassed of my comically pronounced overbite and snaggletooth grin. Like Alcott herself, I enjoyed challenging the boys to footraces.

For Halloween that year I told my mother I wanted to be an "old-fashioned lady." She cobbled a costume from the attic and from church sales: long black dress, long white gloves, ivory fur capelet, white fur muff, black low-heeled pumps, and a broad-brimmed velvet hat spangled with a rhinestone brooch.

I have a snapshot from that night framed on my mantel. Four children standing on a doorstep, my little brother a tiny vampire, all of them looking everywhere but at the camera, while I, the oldest, regal in my finery—the Meg of this ragtag gang—gaze steadily at the lens, my expression serene, even confident. My mouth is clamped closed to conceal my crooked teeth.

Little Women is totally ordinary, but this ordinariness is essential to its magic. Unlike other children's masterpieces of the period—Lewis Carroll's *Alice's Adventures in Wonderland*, Hans Christian Andersen's *The Little Mermaid,* the fairy tales collected by the Brothers Grimm—Alcott's book lured readers not with fantastical adventures and talking animals, but with a realism that was radical in its forthrightness, giving voice to female adolescence. The novel articulates everyday emotions for an audience that is old enough to have experienced them, but still lacks the vocabulary necessary to express the abstractions of heightened consciousness.

At eight years old I could tell my mother that I *hated*

the polyester red turtleneck bodysuit with snaps at the crotch she made me wear with a red plaid kilt for my school picture, but the only tool I owned to convey this opinion was my vehemence. (Also scissors, though infuriatingly, when I tried to plunge the blades into the stretchy fabric, they bounced off. The family album shows she managed to get me into that vile garment after all.) By ten or eleven, I had absorbed enough crude rhetoric to be able to write anguished notes intended to guilt my parents into buying me the brand-name L.L.Bean snow boots I so desperately wanted. (In the end they succumbed, though to fatigue rather than guilt or a change of reasoning.)

At nine, when I encountered *Little Women*, I was somewhere in between. I was still very much a child, disheveled, chatty, completely immersed in imaginary worlds, and quite bossy, making other children perform in the plays I wrote, or listen to me read my stories out loud. But when the school year began, I found myself among the first in fourth grade to develop breasts. I was astonished by the intrusion, embarrassed. I didn't mind being a girl, particularly, but in a deeply inchoate way I understood that childhood was coming to an end and life held in store many more ordeals. Newly self-conscious, I noticed for the first time that my best friends, a pair of fraternal twins with limpid eyes, sweet bow lips, and thick waves tamed with darling barrettes, were what adults called "such pretty girls," and that I wasn't. Once again I lacked the language to express any of this.

It wasn't the first time fiction had presented me with a mirror. I had seen much of myself in Beverly Cleary's Ramona Quimby, and Lucy Maud Montgomery's Anne Shirley, though in that case *too* much—buck-toothed, scrawny, freckled, talkative, blown every which way by emotional gusts. What was the point in reading about myself? I gave up after the first book in the series. At first, *Little Women* seemed the same, offering me Jo, another reflection. A tomboy who writes stories. So what, didn't we all? She even resembled me: "big hands and feet, a fly-away look to her clothes, and the uncomfortable appearance of a girl who was rapidly shooting up into a woman, and didn't like it." Begrudgingly I soldiered on, vaguely annoyed to be saddled with yet another doppelgänger, and increasingly suspicious of Jo's insistence that looks don't matter, when in real life I was beginning to sense that the opposite was true. One afternoon during recess, my teacher gently called me aside. Would I like her to raise the issue of braces with my parents? Until that moment, I hadn't realized that the jokes the other kids made about my teeth weren't meant to be funny, but mean.

Jo also possessed something I didn't: an older sister.

I had never longed for an older sister, I suppose because I was busy being an older sister myself. I took great pride in tending to my younger brother, a towheaded miscreant four years my junior. Meg didn't particularly captivate me either. Did she anyone? Kind, gentle, responsible—the closest thing the book has to a conventional literary heroine—she is yawningly familiar, the quintessential good girl of morality tales and parental remonstrances the world over.

Everything we need to know about her is right there on the first page. Jo grumbles about Christmas not being Christmas without any presents, and Meg, "looking down at her old dress," sighs, "It's so dreadful to be poor!" Just a few pages later, when Meg announces that she's going to give up acting in their "dressing up" frolics, Jo calls her bluff: "You won't stop, I know, as long as you can trail round in a white gown with your hair down, and wear gold-paper jewelry." A bride-to-be already. Soon after, when they're invited to a New Year's Eve party, Meg's first thought is, "now what *shall* we wear?" Vanity, of course, is Meg's one real flaw.

Initially, I deigned to appreciate her in a bland, idle way, for being a good big sister, which I knew full well wasn't always easy. Then the fact of her prettiness sunk in—this I found interesting. When I read that Meg was "very pretty, being plump and fair, with large eyes, plenty of soft brown hair, a sweet mouth, and white hands, of which she was rather vain," I pictured my friends the fraternal twins. What was it like to be pretty? To draw admiration by doing absolutely nothing, as opposed to cajoling others to pay attention to my endless theatrics?

There was also the fact that Meg, a glamorous sixteen, was well past the bodily changes of early adolescence, and untroubled by them. Someone into the breach before me.

What an elixir! A universe so familiar I could smell it (wood smoke, gingerbread, wet wool), yet not without its curious anachronisms (bows on caps, hairnets, toasting forks), which both resonated with my present-day and provided a template for a future self, one I was only then in the process of becoming aware of. And so nine-year-old me continued reading, hovering somewhere between the two elder March sisters, still defined by the qualities of Jo, and wondering if I'd ever be so lucky as to attain those of Meg.

What is it that happens between a woman and her clothes? Virginia Woolf coined the term "frock consciousness" to describe this relationship or frequency or vibration—whatever it is—in a 1925 diary entry. *Mrs. Dalloway* had just been published, and she'd been sitting for a photograph in *Vogue*. "My present reflection," she wrote, "is that people have any number of states of consciousness: & I should like to investigate the party consciousness, the frock consciousness &c. These states are very difficult . . . I'm always coming back to it . . . Still I cannot get at what I mean."

She wanted to unpack the simultaneous outward-inward nature of clothing—the fact that what we wear is a visible, tactile membrane between our private and public selves that expresses who we think we are or who we wish to be, while also affecting how others feel about us, a curious feedback loop of self-perception. In a wonderful essay about Woolf's inquiry, the scholar Rosemary Hill points out that Clarissa Dalloway's favorite dress "is both distinctive and yet suitable," which is "what many women want from their clothes, to stand out and to fit in to the same degree at the same time." When I read that line I silently applauded its accuracy. Is that not exactly what I'm trying to accomplish nearly every time I dress to leave the house?

Woolf was in her early forties when she began thinking about this subject, which is the age I began looking closely at it myself. I don't think this is a coincidence. By middle age, as our bodies submit to change yet again—the anti-puberty—we've achieved enough distance from our corporality to be able to regard it with more dispassion than was possible back when our hormones overrode all else. As Alcott put it in her "Happy Women" essay, "After a somewhat tempestuous voyage, she is glad to find herself in a quiet haven whence she can look back upon her vanished youth and feel that though the blossom time of life is past, a little fruit remains to ripen in the early autumn coming on." (Note that she was only thirty-six when she wrote this.)

In that essay, Alcott evaluates the looks of the three

other spinsters she writes about. One is "pretty," one "attractive," one "plain." Notably, she doesn't ascribe judgment to herself. How could she know, really? This question—"Am I plain, or am I pretty?"—seems to me central to frock consciousness. We have all seen love and hate transfigure a face, when we are doing the looking; recall Mr. Darcy saying in *Pride and Prejudice* that knowing Elizabeth Bennett better made her seem the most handsome woman of his acquaintance. Likewise, the sensation of wearing the "right" clothes—right in the sense that Rosemary Hill pinpoints, right in the manner of my fourth-grade Halloween costume—imparts a self-possession that transcends being looked at, or at least renders the judgment of others meaningless.

"Am I plain, or am I pretty?" I think this question was a little easier to answer in Alcott's time. When women had so few resources at their disposal to alter their appearance, and had to rely exclusively on their so-called god-given features, the demarcation was strict, but clear. All those severe buns and strict center parts. No such thing as lipstick or mascara—not among the respectable women of New England, that is.

And so there it was: Meg was pretty. Jo wasn't. Harsh,

sure, and we all know it's not as neat as all that, that beauty is in the eye of the beholder, that sometimes physical beauty doesn't even matter. After all, it was Jo who not only won Laurie's heart, and had the presence of mind and self-assurance to reject him, but also went down in history as the most influential of the March sisters, inspiring the likes of Simone de Beauvoir and Patti Smith to become writers—the ultimate ugly duckling-turned-swan. Before I learned that Alcott was a spinster, not a mother, and returned to *Little Women*, I didn't even think of Meg.

As it turned out, imagining myself into Meg's prettiness as a child had taken me only so far; biology is brutal like that. Braces came in sixth grade, pimples in seventh, and both remained all through high school. My mother instilled in me second-wave feminism's antipathy toward makeup and rolled her eyes when I expressed Meg-like longings for fashionable clothes (though she did buy me more than a few). She, too, had grown up plain, but in the conformist 1950s, when beauty was still a woman's greatest asset, plainness verboten, and girdles and hair rollers nonnegotiable. She wanted to raise me free of the painful strictures of dressing to fit in. I trusted her.

She was smarter than the other mothers. I felt lucky to follow in her footsteps.

In the chapter "Castles in the Air," when Laurie and the March sisters fantasize about their futures, and Meg realizes that, unlike Jo and Amy, she doesn't have a vocation to help her achieve "a lovely house, full of all sorts of luxurious things," Laurie points out that she does have something else—her face. "Wait and see if it doesn't bring you something worth having," he says. My mother wanted me to know I was so much more than whatever I looked like.

Everyone assured me that college would be different, but it wasn't, not really. Pretty continued to evade me. I both did and didn't mind. Simply living inside of a female body taught me the discomfort of being looked at, and for the most part, being plain seemed a welcome reprieve from all that. Like Jo, it gave me control. It forced me to center my appeal inside of myself. I recognized prettiness in others, I admired it, I occasionally envied it, but mostly I accepted that they were one way and I was another. Boys liked me well enough as I was, which helped.

It probably took me longer than it should have to

understand that biology is only one part of the story. "Say what your beauty means to you or your plainness, and what is your relation to the everchanging and turning world of gloves and shoes and stuffs," Woolf writes in "A Room of One's Own." Once upon a time, I took stock of my plainness, and I accepted it. Or so I thought. Not until my early thirties did I reckon with the "world of gloves and shoes and stuffs."

It wasn't my first dress fiasco, but it was my first of any significance. At thirty-three I'd taken an editorial position at a glossy lifestyle magazine in Times Square, where I learned that whatever attractiveness I possessed could be improved upon: my blotchy skin and acne scars could be concealed with foundation, my lank locks enlivened with a good (and expensive) haircut, my short legs lengthened with high heels. The discovery that it was within my power to enhance my appearance was when things got confusing.

Until then, I'd bought my clothes on sale or secondhand, proud of my thrift, proud even to cultivate desires for garments based mainly on their affordability; my wardrobe was a collection of misfits and underdogs that had, thanks to my munificence, found a home, or so went my pretense. Now that I was making real money, I could walk into a shop, fall in love with a dress or a sweater on its merits alone, and suddenly own it, just like that. I'd assumed such freedom would bring me pleasure; I hadn't anticipated the complications. For one, I couldn't let go of the internal agitation it caused me to spend money—a small tightening in the chest, almost a shortness of breath, followed by a massive distrust in my purchase, and an overwhelming urge to return it. A Massachusetts puritan to the bone. Worse, wearing something that fit the way it was intended to, or was a color that flattered my complexion, or any number of details that make a garment suit a woman and enhance her attractiveness, made me deeply uncomfortable, as if I were trying to be something I wasn't.

At the magazine, someone came up with the phrase "frock shock" to describe those mornings one or the other of us was late to work because we'd been standing paralyzed in front of our closets incapable of choosing what to wear. It was a ridiculous problem to have, but the fact that I wasn't alone in it was a true comfort.

My boss, Claire (not her real name), was a wealthy,

extroverted woman with an aggressive sense of humor who didn't like me very much. In meetings she'd cry out, "Bolick! Say something! You creep me out being so quiet!" and I'd explain, again, that I just don't think very well when I'm around other people, that once I was back alone at my desk I would be able to come up with ideas. I wanted to be better, I just didn't know how. My earnest ineptitude intensified her frustration, creating a dismaying static we couldn't get past.

It wasn't only my personality she disliked. There was also my relationship with her college friend Noah (not his real name, either), an art historian I'd met long before I'd started the job. He was the sort of person who cultivated a cult of scarcity, keeping himself consistently slightly unavailable to the people in his life, so that everyone always wanted more and envied everyone else their share. My indeterminable status made me even more threatening to my boss than I would have been otherwise. I wasn't Noah's girlfriend—he made that clear—but neither was I his friend, because we'd been sleeping together off and on for years, nor was I his mistress, because we were both unpartnered. In the beginning, I found the unclarity of it all intoxicating, but over time I grew to resent it. I wanted to be one thing or the other: friend or girlfriend. He refused. I was in a trap—but a trap of my own making. If I could only not want him, I could be free. Try as I might, I couldn't not want him. I suspected that if I were prettier, things would be different.

As Noah's not-girlfriend/not-friend, I rarely spent time with his actual friends, so when he invited me to the summer party that my boss was hosting for the magazine he was breaking code. Unlike the occasional staff event we were all encouraged to attend, this one was exclusively for top executives, advertisers, industry insiders, and Claire's successful friends. She had asked Noah to be a guest at her table, and he had asked me to be his plus one. My breath caught when he asked. Did he know what he was doing? It was the modern-day equivalent of bringing the scullery maid to her employer's society ball. I saw instantly that he did know, very much. My presence at the party would be a thorn in my boss's side, and that was the point.

Obviously, I accepted. I had no idea why he wanted to get under her skin, and I didn't care, because finally I was getting the social validation I'd craved. That it came at the cost of Claire disliking me more than she already did seemed a small price. There were even flashes, during those two weeks until the party, when I felt a sort of diabolical delight in the discomfort it must be causing her. Mostly, though, I worried over what to wear. My work wardrobe was a vast improvement over what it had once been, but "cocktail attire"—as suggested on the official printed invitation—remained beyond me. That weekend I unearthed the blue cotton dress I'd worn to my brother's rehearsal dinner and ironed out the wrinkles. I doubted it was right for this occasion, but I hoped it would do.

When I returned to *Little Women* as an adult, knowing what I do now about Alcott's opinion of marriage, I was eager to see how she'd treated Meg's betrothal to John Brooke, which was clearly the most—indeed, the only—important event in Meg's life (along with becoming a mother).

Ah, clever Alcott. Even here she subverts expectations. Rather than give readers the satisfaction of ending part one with a white wedding, she saves it for part two's second chapter—and she breezes right through it. That chapter is among the shortest in the entire book. Moreover, aside from moving the plot forward, it's largely a callback to Meg's most significant chapter, in part one, about the time she goes off to spend "a fortnight of novelty and pleasure" with her rich friend Annie Moffat.

"Meg goes to Vanity Fair" is Meg's only departure from the bosom of family. Unlike Amy and Jo, who both were given the chance to demonstrate Alcott's belief that young women should live for a significant period of time on their own to discover themselves, Meg is granted only these two weeks. Fittingly, the chapter title refers to the fair held in the frivolous town of Vanity in John Bunyan's *The Pilgrim's Progress*, a favorite text of both the March and Alcott families. (It's possible that Alcott had also read Thackeray's 1848 novel *Vanity Fair*.) Packing her humble frocks for the trip, Meg says, impatiently, "I wonder if I shall *ever* be happy enough to have real lace on my clothes, and bows on my caps?"

The problem of vanity isn't entirely beyond the comprehension of a nine-year-old girl. I knew it well from Snow White's plight; were her stepmother less vain, she wouldn't have tried to get her killed. Class disparity was equally legible. I understood that Cinderella was poor,

Prince Charming rich, and that the right dress would blind him to this discrepancy (the economic aspect of frock consciousness exemplified); that if all went well she'd marry him, thus becoming rich herself; and that being rich was perforce a good thing, possibly the best thing, better than being good, because clearly kindness alone wasn't doing Cinderella any favors.

The subtler implications of Meg's mini-adventure, however, were lost on me. I glossed over the pointed description of the Moffats as "kindly people, in spite of the frivolous life they led." Like Meg, I imagined it would be "agreeable to fare sumptuously, drive in a fine carriage, wear her best frock every day, and do nothing but enjoy herself." (Well, had I known then what a frock was, I wouldn't have liked that part.) When I read that Meg and her three friends "shopped, walked, rode, and called all day; went to the theatres and operas," I pictured the preteen girls I saw in my own hometown, free to go wherever they wanted unchaperoned, which I would also be at liberty to do in three years, when I turned twelve.

Nor did I understand the shame Meg felt over having only two dresses, so new was I at comparing myself with others. And so I thrilled at the chapter's apogee, when the kindly Belle Moffat, Annie's sister, offers to loan Meg her "sweet blue silk" to wear to their final fancy fête. The evening of, Belle and her maid crimp and curl Meg's hair, shower her with "some fragrant powder," redden her lips with "coralline salve"—after that Meg draws the line: no rouge—and lace her into the tight-fitting, low-cut, sky-blue gown. A full set of jewelry, a cluster of rosebuds, and high-heeled blue silk boots from France complete the effect. Everyone deems her "a little beauty."

Meg had always known herself to be pretty. But now when she looks in the mirror she sees something else—a "fashion plate," as she later confesses to her mother. For a long several minutes, heart beating, feeling "as if her 'fun' had really begun at last," she stands alone, admiring her transformation. This is where Alcott twists the knife. She compares Meg to the jackdaw in Aesop's famous fable, who, after envying the peacocks' splendid feathers, sticks a bunch of their "borrowed plumes" into his own plain black tail—then struts among his fellow jackdaws, fooling nobody but himself. As if heeding Alcott's warning, here Meg pauses for a moment, afraid to go down to the party "so queer and stiff, and half-dressed." But quickly enough she summons her courage and sails into the drawing-rooms, where she successfully passes as a fine lady and enjoys herself.

Until, that is, she looks across the room and sees Laurie, "staring at her with undisguised surprise, and disapproval also." Suddenly self-conscious again, wishing she'd worn her old dress after all, she nonetheless crosses the room to greet him. He refuses to meet her eyes. He admits that he's "quite afraid" of her, looking "so grown-up, and unlike yourself," then adds that he doesn't like "fuss and feathers." Hurt, she tells him off, but when she huffs away she overhears a conversation in which she's referred to as "nothing but a doll, to-night." Cooling her cheeks by the window, she muses, "I wish I'd been sensible, and worn my own things; then I should not have disgusted other people, or felt so uncomfortable and ashamed myself." Laurie apologizes and they dance, but later, when he catches her drinking champagne, he tries to shame her again. This time, "with an affected little laugh," she shuts him down: "I'm not Meg, to-night; I'm 'a doll,' who does all sorts of crazy things. To-morrow I shall put away my 'fuss and feathers,' and be desperately good again."

It's a captivating moment of double consciousness. For the first time, Meg has looked in the mirror and seen how gorgeous she can be, how very like the illustrated fashion plates she's heretofore admired in magazines. The sumptuous clothes are both costume and passpor; passing as someone she's not, she's free to assume behaviors she never would otherwise. And yet, having at last achieved her long-held desire for lace and bows on her clothes—albeit borrowed—she spends her night of glory not in unmitigated triumph, like Cinderella, but demeaned like the jackdaw, careening between compliments and insults, excitement and embarrassment, wholly at the mercy of how others experience her manifest beauty, and ultimately deprived of her own pleasure.

Did Alcott intend Meg's vanity as punishment for not having pursuits of her own, other than to someday marry, and have a nice house and clothes? Or was she lobbing a warning about the pernicious underside of upward mobility? Of the four sisters, only Meg is old enough to be off navigating fraught social spaces. In Alcott's time, if a young woman from a poor family appreciated nice things, the only way to get them was through marriage or prostitution. Unsurprisingly, perhaps, it was the barely middle-class Alcott, not the upper-class Woolf, who recognized this economic aspect of frock consciousness. Maybe Alcott wasn't punishing Meg so much as admitting that, lacking the freedoms granted to men, many women rely on other means to express their more limited range of powers. It was her hope that Meg—and all the rest of us—would find a better way.

Some memories progress in stages, instead of appearing all at once. We can't always know what is happening as it happens; if we're lucky, we remember later, at which point our recollection is informed by the knowledge we've since accrued. It's not that we misremember, necessarily, or not always. It's that in the act of remembering we can't help seeing the event in a way that we couldn't when it first took place. It's a useful process. A retrospective wisdom.

Is it possible to say that during my dress fiasco I had a cellular memory of Meg's shame over the blue silk dress? I don't know. It feels too romantic. And yet I do believe that books seep into us and change us in ways we can't keep track of. At nine, I breezed through Meg's fortnight with the Moffats, only taking in the elements that made quick sense to me. Then, many years later, I experienced the same event in my own life, without remembering hers. After that, more years passed, until I finally read *Little Women* again and revisited Meg's frock shock on the page, but this time through the scrim of my own memory, as if overlaying Alcott's words was a sheet of tracing paper on which I'd sketched my own episode. This time around it was a dual experience: Meg's and my own.

The morning of my boss's party I arrived at work to find a garment bag laid across my desk. It was customary for Claire to "call in" clothes from designers to wear to big events, and at first I assumed this had something to do with that—that they were hers, somehow misplaced—but when I looked inside I saw two dresses in my size. I ran to her office to thank her, but she wasn't there, so I ran instead to the bathroom to try them on.

The first was very "me," something I would have picked out myself. Prim, retro, it was made of a slightly stiff fabric, almost a brocade, woven with big gold and silver triangles. The bodice had a high crew neck and short sleeves, and the skirt was an A-line that hit at the knee. Or, it was supposed to. To look right it would need to be taken up several inches. The other was made of a black silk jersey that slunk in my hands like a cat. Once on, it clung to every curve I had. The neckline plunged to my sternum.

I stared at myself in the mirror. I had never seen myself like this—so unapologetically sexy, in the contemporary sense, like an actress on the red carpet. I looked and looked. I couldn't take my eyes off myself.

At that moment the fashion editor walked into the bathroom, unsurprised; she'd been the one to guess my size, and what styles might suit me.

"Looks good," she said, glancing at me, before disappearing into a stall, "but you'll definitely need some bronzer on your chest."

I took in my very white, freckled décolletage and knew it didn't matter, that I'd never wear this dress anyhow.

At 5:00 P.M. I raced back to Brooklyn and straight to the tailor to beg her to hem the gold-and-silver dress in an hour. She kindly agreed. At home, I showered and blew my hair dry, twisted it into a loose chignon, applied makeup, then got down on my hands and knees and went hunting through my closet for the black heels I'd

worn to my brother's wedding. After exactly sixty minutes had passed I dashed out to the tailor's, retrieved the
gold-and-silver dress, ran back home, put it on, touched
up my lipstick one more time, grabbed the doorknob—
and paused. Without letting myself think I turned
around, pulled off the gold-and-silver dress, stepped into
the black one, zipped it up, grabbed the doorknob again,
and left my apartment.

By the time I reached the corner to find a cab, I could
barely contain my anxiety. What a fool I'd been! How
could I possibly go out in public looking like this—so
attention-grabbing, so conspicuous, so one-note "sexy"?
I looked ridiculous! I had to go back and change! Just
then, a taxi pulled up. Heart pounding, I dove inside,
gave the driver the address, on the far west side of Man-
hattan, and telephoned my brother. When he picked up I
was nearly hyperventilating. "What is it? What is it?" he
kept asking, and I had no idea how to explain.

"I'm on my way to a party," I said, to allay his alarm,
though saying the words out loud only made my situation more inexplicable. I was on my way to a party,
wearing a designer dress, in a cab no less, and I couldn't
breathe. My brother, bless him, stayed on the line until

I'd arrived. I paid the fare, stepped out of the cab. The venue overlooked the Hudson River, orange with the lowering sun.

The walls resembled glass waves. I could see inside to the party, already in full swing. I wished for a coat, an excuse to visit the cloakroom, a buffer between apprehending the party and becoming subsumed. Instead, I pulled open the glass door and walked straight in, got a drink, found Noah in the crowd.

He wore dark jeans, a charcoal suit jacket, a white dress shirt, black shoes.

He looked me up and down. He didn't look at me so much as look through me. His expression was one of mild disdain. At last, he spoke.

"Well, well," he said, archly, cocking an eyebrow. "If someone didn't take 'cocktail attire' to the next level."

I froze, smothered in shame. I had tried to be something I wasn't, and I hadn't succeeded. I would never be pretty. I would never fit in. I would always be the scrawny girl with buckteeth and lank hair, the misfit with odd thoughts and the wrong clothes. He would never love me the way that I wanted.

While rereading *Little Women* I was struck by the section in the chapter "Tender Troubles" that goes on and on about Jo's "repulsive" pillow, known as "the sausage." Alcott describes the March family sofa as "a regular patriarch of a sofa—long, broad, well-cushioned and low. A trifle shabby." Jo claimed one corner as her own, and monitored her territory with a hard, round pillow "covered with prickly horse-hair, and furnished with a knobby button at each end." When "the sausage" is standing up, Laurie is free to lounge as much as he'd like, "but if it laid flat across the sofa, woe to the man, woman or child who dared disturb it." It's a strange, amusing passage, one of the rare portions of the book that breaks the otherwise steady narrative pacing, and the details themselves feel far too specific and exhaustively drawn to be made up. When I finished the book, I traveled to the house in Concord where Alcott wrote it, and learned that I'd been onto something, that the pillow was real.

The pillow on display, apparently the original, is a standard cylindrical bolster, maybe two feet long, covered in a russety-brown velvet. The guide explained that it was known in the family as Alcott's "mood pillow," and used to signal her emotional state while she was busy writing. When the pillow was up, all was well, and visitors to her room upstairs were welcome. When the pillow was down, it meant she was having a difficult time with her work and wanted to be left alone.

I stood for as long as the tour allowed, just looking at the pillow. It was such a homely thing, and yet totally exceptional, a golden key, a personification of Alcott's consciousness. Alcott was rare enough among women of her time for being a professional writer; here was evidence that her family supported her so completely that even her moods were given the run of the house. No wonder she didn't want to marry. As if the social role of "wife" weren't oppressive enough, was there a man alive who could have stepped back and let her continue on as she had? For her, the struggle wasn't merely to reconcile work and love, autonomy and intimacy, but to protect her own individuality, which was free to flourish in her family of origin, and would surely be inhibited if she ever left to start a family of her own. This, I now saw, was why she had Jo marry Friedrich Bhaer—Alcott couldn't find such a progressive Prince Charming in real life, but she could invent him.

My head was so full of these thoughts when the tour concluded, in the gift shop, that when I saw a book titled

Moods I almost didn't believe my eyes. Was the gift shop reading my mind?

It was Alcott's first novel for adults, which she began at age twenty-seven, long before *Little Women* and even "Happy Women." Sarah Elbert writes in her introduction that the book is important for raising "a personal and a social question: how could a woman marry and still develop her own unique gifts?" Alcott's answer, of course, is that she can't. The book's heroine, Faith Dane, like her creator, chooses to remain a spinster.

The stifling confines of gender and social roles, frock consciousness and party consciousness, feminism—so many of Alcott's themes presage Virginia Woolf's preoccupations. Had Woolf read *Little Women*? Once I finished rereading, I burned to know. After all, their lives overlapped. Woolf was six years old when Alcott died in 1888, a full two decades after the book became a sensation in America. Plausibly, some grown-up in young Woolf's deeply literary orbit could have given it to her as a present.

I reached out to three scholars of English literature— Elaine Showalter, Emma Claire Sweeney, and Ellen Tremper. They in turn checked the indexes of all of

Woolf's published works, including diaries and letters, and didn't find a single reference to Alcott. I was careful about this, covering my bases, because I wanted to be sure. I wanted to be able to say, without a shadow of a doubt, that English literature would be different if Woolf had known that in her own time lived a woman so like herself. Had Woolf read Alcott's exploration of frock consciousness, she might have simply picked up the baton and kept running with it, rather than grope toward the subject herself, and the rest of us would be even further along than we are now in understanding our own relationships to our clothes.

Meg had fashion plates to look at in magazines, but she definitely didn't have a camera, or of course the internet, and as such she would have never stumbled onto a photograph immortalizing her night of frock shock a decade after the fact, the way I did. I can't remember how I came to find it. But there I am, wearing the slinky black dress for all the world to see. And here's the thing: I don't look remotely as I'd remembered. Sure, the neckline is deeper than I'd wear even now, but with my low black heels, chignon, and eyeglasses perched on top of my head, I hardly look like the overdressed hussy Noah made me feel myself to be.

I've written in the past about how I'd been wrong to spend my young womanhood thinking there were only two ways to be—single or married—when in fact here in the twenty-first century most of us live in the vast space in between. Ours is an era of delayed marriage, sexual promiscuity, asserted celibacy, sanctioned polyamory, serial monogamy—anything goes, from our romantic arrangements to our hemlines. Now the trick is to update the internal scripts in our heads to match these new realities.

And so it is with plain vs. pretty. The message I took from Alcott and my mother was that pretty is a prison. If, like Meg, you are pretty, you can't also be a writer, or an artist. If, like Amy, you are almost pretty but not quite, you are eternally vexed by the one feature that doomed you. If you are plain, like Jo and my mother and me, and maybe even Alcott, you are free.

But I was mistaken. Meg and Jo and Amy and Beth were neither morality tales nor real people. They were fictional characters drawn from life to embody different aspects of the female experience. *Little Women* has endured across the centuries because it invites the reader to imagine herself into a variety of personalities, both in real time while reading, and afterward, in reflection. As a girl I was a Jo who never became a Meg and in the process became something else. Ultimately, I am all of the sisters. I am Marmee and the aunts. I am even the writer herself. Books enlarge us. We read, and we move forward.

We live, and we're held back. I allied myself with my mother's plainness because it was the path she bequeathed me, and taking it gave us closeness. But doing so foreclosed my ability to discover my own fluidity. As with everything else in life, I had to learn my own relationship to myself, and choose how to interact with the vagaries of my era. Is makeup enfeebling or empowering? I honestly can't decide. But continuing to live inside of that question, instead of fixing myself within yet another either/or binary—whether plain vs. pretty, friend vs. girlfriend, single vs. married—is part of what it means to be a woman in our time. Indecision and irresolution are our modernity.

All these years later I can see that Claire was doing me a favor when she loaned me that slinky black dress. Just as Belle Moffat encouraged Meg to try on a dress that belonged to a different type of life, to a different version of Meg, Claire gave me the chance to see myself as I might never otherwise, allowing me to expand my individuality in a way that Noah (and in Meg's case, Laurie) couldn't abide. I believe that the most we can ask from the people in our lives is that, no matter what, when they see us grow or change in an unexpected direction, they stand aside and let it happen.

JENNY ZHANG ON JO

DOES GENIUS BURN, JO?

"Genius; don't you wish you could give it to me, Laurie?"

FROM THE MOMENT I learned English—my second language—I decided I was destined for genius and it would be discovered through my writing—my brilliant, brilliant writing. Until then, I had to undergo training, the way a world-class athlete might prepare for the Olympics; so I did what any budding literary marvel desperate to get to the glory and praise stage of her career would do—I read and read and read and then imitated my idols in hope that my talents would one day catch up to my tastes. At age ten, I gave up picture books and took the leap into chapter books, but continued to seek out the girly subjects that alone interested me. Any story involving an abandoned young girl, left to survive this harsh, bitter world on her own, was catnip to my writerly ambitions. Like the literary characters I loved, the protagonists in my own early efforts at writing were plucky, determined, unconventional girls, which was how I saw myself. They often acted impetuously, were prone to bouts of sulking and extreme mood swings, sweet one minute and sour the next. I always gave my heroines happy endings—they were all wunderkinds who were wildly successful in their artistic pursuits and, on top of it, found true, lasting love with a perfect man. I was a girl on the cusp of adolescence, but I had already fully bought into the fantasy that women should and could have it all.

On one of my family's weekly trips to Costco, I found a gorgeous illustrated copy of *Little Women* by Louisa May Alcott, a book I had seen and written off every time I went to the library, repelled by the word *women*. Unlike the girl heroines I loved, a *woman* was something I dreaded becoming, a figure bound up in expectations of sacrifice and responsibility. A woman had to face reality and give up her foolish childish dreams. And what was reality for a woman but the life my mother—the best woman I knew—had? And what did she have but a mountain of responsibilities—to me, to my father, to my younger brother, to her parents, to my father's parents, to her friends, to my father's friends, to their friends' parents, to her bosses, to her coworkers, and so on? Her accomplishments were bound up in other people, and her work was literally emotional, as she was expected to be completely attuned to everyone else's feelings. She worked service jobs where she was required to absorb the anger of complaining customers and never betray any frustration of her own. Her livelihood depended on being giving and kind all of the time, suppressing her less sunny emotions into a perpetually soaked rag that she sometimes wrung out on my father and me.

My mother had apparently wanted to be a writer when she was a young girl too. She loved reading novels and writing stories, but she continually repeated to me the same proselytizing refrain: everyone has to grow up and be responsible for others. And one day you will too, she forecasted; or, maybe she was trying to hex me. She wanted me to stop thinking of myself as some great exception. She believed the numbers didn't lie—if something was popular, then that thing must be really good. That was her credo in life; if it applied to restaurants, it certainly applied to marriage and family. One had to do the expected thing, or else one was fucked. The odds were much higher that a young girl might one day find a husband and start a family of her own than become a famous writer. My mother believed no matter how miserable marriage and kids might be, it was guaranteed to be better than the misery of being childless and unpartnered. Better to be normal than to try to be extraordinary, she told me again and again.

Her and my father's vision of womanhood was a nightmare to me. According to them, the best possible outcome was that I become a dentist. A dentist! Someone whose entire job was to look inside other people's mouths. Whose line of work inspired fear, dread, and procrastination. I wanted to inspire action, write poems that transported the reader into the realm of magic, be the embodiment of Rilke's *you must change your life,* and nothing less. When I nixed my parents' ambition that I become a dentist, they suggested an alternative—law—quick to add they didn't mean the lawyers on TV who went to trial and made impassioned arguments against the ills of racism and corporate greed, but the ones who sat around in the office all day completing paperwork. That was the dream of the good life my parents had for me: a safe job where I didn't have to overexert myself.

Passion was bad. Routine, clerical tasks, low-risk paper-pushing that could be reliably repeated over and over again until I retired and lived out the rest of my life through careful budgeting of my retirement savings, was good. And of course, I was to find a man with the same values, marry, and procreate with him before my eggs dried up and I was nothing but a shriveled hag.

Why not just end life right here and now? I thought every time my parents brought it up. Better to die tragically young having experienced some shit than to make it to old age bored out of your mind. Perhaps there was someone who wanted the life my parents advocated for, could imagine being happy in it, could even take pleasure from achieving such milestones, but it wasn't me. The picture my parents painted of my eventual ascension into womanhood was a prison. I wanted to stay a girl for as long as I could—it was the last stop before I had to annihilate all my dreams and get real.

When I finally read *Little Women*, it was out of boredom. My parents left me in the Costco book aisle for the better part of an hour, during which I devoured more than half the book. It was a paperback edition but the pages felt like heavy, quality cardstock. The cover showed the March sisters in wide-brimmed hats trimmed with ribbon, delicately brandishing walking sticks. Meg was depicted in a Peter Pan–collared lavender dress with vertical white stripes, Jo in an unadorned navy dress with a priestlike white collar, Beth in a faded yellow pinstriped dress, and little Amy in a skyblue sailor dress. Jo was the decidedly plain one, the one who clearly took no joy in having a beauty regimen. Under the bright warehouse lights, to my surprise, I was immediately enamored with the story of sisterhood and genteel struggle, enticed by the exoticism of a tale set against the backdrop of the Civil War—a period of time I could not fathom outside of history books—with its strange touchstones like only having enough money for lobster salad, scheming to possess a large quantity of pickled limes and secretly sucking them at school, and lunches composed of cold tongue. Though I had no sisters of my own, the story of four sisters raised by their self-sacrificing mother to be just as self-sacrificing despite repeated dips into the dramatic, self-involved throes of adolescence and puberty was incredibly familiar to me.

I should have identified with Jo, who possesses her creator's best traits in spades (individuality, fearlessness, resourcefulness, and creativity), while the more trying aspects of Louisa May Alcott's personality (the volatile temper and mood swings that would most likely be diagnosed as some kind of mood or personality disorder today) were mitigated by the author's pen. After all, Jo March has always been the fan favorite, the little woman everyone thinks herself to be, the clear front man of the four-piece band, the one who hogged all the charisma and daring, the only one of the sisters whose vision of what a woman's life should and could entail doesn't seem so miserably dated today, the one character who has been cited by a roll call of prominent women writers[1] as inspirational and as essential to their own artistic and feminist development, not to mention all the women whose names and lives were not famous enough to be recorded for posterity but who nonetheless were altered by Jo March. In the context of literature written for young girls, Jo stands out. She is the rare fictional teenage girl who prefers the dirtiness of adventure to

1. bell hooks, Susan Sontag, Ursula K. Le Guin, Simone de Beauvoir, Gloria Steinem, Jhumpa Lahiri, Patti Smith, Nora Ephron, Margaret Atwood, Doris Lessing, Zadie Smith, Erica Jong, Elizabeth Alexander, J. K. Rowling, and Maxine Hong Kingston, to name a few.

the cleanliness of order, who sees no romance in being tethered to a man, who rolls her eyes at the material inheritances promised by marriage, who would rather work her ass off to support her family through her writing than be saved by a man with money, who spends the majority of the book bucking the patriarchal fetish that women eternally sacrifice their own pleasure and efface their own desires in the service of men. She is the character that most young girls who read *Little Women* are proud to identify with—and there I was, twelve years old, a self-professed "rebel" and "writing prodigy" who decided by the end of the first page that there was nobody I detested more than Jo March. Her boyishness, her impetuousness, her obliviousness, her agility at all types of masculine movement and her clumsiness at feminine preening, her utter lack of interest in the romantic attentions of men—in particular, her best friend and boy-next-door Laurie, who was a dreamboat to me, feminine in his name, teen girly in his adoration and unrequited love for Jo and even more so in his reaction to being rejected (not so vaguely threatening suicide, flinging his body around in despair, wailing dramatically, "I *can't* love any one else; and I'll never forget you, Jo, never! never!")—her ideals, her stubbornness, her independence, her utter lack of giving a fuck when it came to adhering to gender norms, everything about Jo repulsed me.

I should have identified with Jo, the only one of the sisters who not only wants to be a genius but by the end of the book is still in the running to be one.[2] When playing a cheeky game of truth, Laurie asks Jo, "What do you most wish for?" to which Jo replies disingenuously, "A pair of boot-lacings." Laurie calls her on her bluff, "Not a true answer; you must say what you really do want most," and Jo fires back, "'Genius; don't you wish you could give it to me, Laurie?' and she shyly smiled in his disappointed face," reminding the reader that she's the

---

2. By contrast, Amy March, the youngest and most spoiled March sister, who often serves as the foil to Jo in the book, getting the opportunities that are denied to Jo, is decidedly *not* in the running for genius. When we check back in on the March sisters in part two of *Little Women*, Amy's chapter begins with extreme shade: "It takes people a long time to learn the difference between talent and genius, especially ambitious young men and women. Amy was learning this distinction through much tribulation; for, mistaking enthusiasm for inspiration, she attempted every branch of art with youthful audacity."

only one of the four March sisters who desires something that no man can give her. What she desires is to burn with creativity, awaken the genius lying dormant in her soul. Later when Laurie confesses his love for her, Jo is baffled, makes it clear she does not reciprocate, and even goes so far as to say she doubts she'll ever marry and give it all up for some guy. Laurie doesn't buy it. No woman can be happy on her own; they all end up finding a man they are willing "to live and die for," so why, why, why not him?

Rather than applaud Jo and her wherewithal to choose herself over the love of a good (and hot) (and wealthy) man at a time when women were structurally denied power and resources and had few options outside of marriage, I was horrified. How selfish, I thought, my criticism mirroring my mother's jabs at me whenever I announced my intentions to be a writer, not someone's mother. She's never going to do better than Laurie! I fumed. What does he even see in her? I wondered. What made her think she could be free like a boy? What made a poor girl like her think she could act like a person with money?

Was my reaction because I saw parts of myself in Jo

and didn't like what I saw? Did other people see me the way I saw her—annoying, delusional, unwilling to grow up, stubbornly clinging to her childish dreams? It was through Jo that I finally tapped into the mindset of the very people I had been rebelling against: my parents. And in some sneaky way, it was Jo's journey in *Little Women* that gave me insight into why my parents were so hell-bent on conforming. They had lived longer and survived more than I had and knew much more than I did about how much this world punishes those who don't fall in line.

"I get so savage, I could hurt any one, and enjoy it."

Growing up in Shanghai, I was a happy, extroverted, outgoing child. For the first four years of my life, I was the Amy March of my large, extended family. Everything I did was worthy of praise. Distant relatives and friends came from all over to see me, the golden child, the blessed baby. In the presence of company, I was serene and lovable. Once alone with my family, I was hyper. At nine months I was speaking in full sentences, by ten I was singing and dancing. I loved to entertain, most of all by telling stories, and as with Jo, made-up stories were often more real to me than my actual lived life. Finding preschool to be a bore, I came home and told my family that our class had gone to the zoo and I had been chosen to ride on the back of an elephant. Like Jo, I loved to direct, putting on theatrical performances for my family filled with song and dance. I saw the world and everyone in it as a potential audience for my art.

The blithe, unearned confidence that radiated from my little soul abruptly died when I immigrated to New York. Suddenly language was stripped from me, no one clapped for me anymore when I spoke. My lack of proficiency in English was at best pitiful, at worst annoying. I had been muted; there was no longer any evidence I could entertain or dazzle. I was not yet five, and I had already undergone an identity crisis. The sweetness I had always been praised for was losing ground to something that little girls were not supposed to feel—anger.

By the end of my first year in America, I had passed out of ESL, but I hadn't passed out of feeling self-conscious every time I spoke. In this new phase of my life, if I wanted to speak, I wrote it down instead. That was where I was the least inhibited, the least clumsy, that was the only space where I was not treated as accented, or worse—broken. I decided to give up on my dream of being a world-renowned entertainer; instead I would be a writer. To say nothing of my delusions of grandeur, there was an even less noble reason motivating my pivot to the written word—I wanted to exact vengeance on everyone who had ever wronged me, underestimated me, or decided on the basis of my face that I was uninteresting, unworthy, and unremarkable. What better *I'll show you* than to become a massively successful published author? What better revenge than to have the last word? Nothing lit a fire under my ass quite like wanting to prove my haters wrong. Nothing gave me a greater sense of power than to recast my life into fiction. Writing was a kind of alchemy; it had the power to turn the garbage of the past into gold.

It has been well documented that much of *Little Women* drew on Louisa's actual family and upbringing. Meg, Jo, Beth, and Amy were modeled after Louisa and her three sisters, and the girls' mother, Marmee, was based on Abba, the overworked matriarch of the Alcott family who ran herself ragged to do what her husband, Bronson Alcott—an educator, writer, abolitionist, and reformer who started several progressive schools and a utopian agrarian community (all these enterprises foundered for one reason or another)—could not do: support the family and keep them afloat. The family often went hungry and suffered through the brutal New England winters as a consequence of Bronson's idealism, which led to practices such as refusing to work for wages, observing a kind of veganism that proscribed the growing and eating of root vegetables in favor of the consumption of "aspiring vegetables" that grew up toward the sun, and no wearing of cotton, silk, or wool because they were products of slave labor and capitalism. The poverty that plagued Louisa's upbringing (in the first twenty-five years of her life, her family moved more than thirty times) was given a much rosier treatment on the page. The suffering the March girls underwent while their father was away serving as a chaplain in the Civil War was honorable and bearable. In the first chapter they give up their Christmas breakfast to a poor, starving family of six and happily return to their home to bulk up on their own goodness in addition to some bread and milk. Our hearts are meant to be warmed by this anecdote of Christmas cheer, but in reality the Alcotts themselves often relied on handouts from others, and often went through long stretches with nothing to eat besides bread, water, and the occasional apple.

Louisa herself was prone to frequent mood swings and an unpredictable temper. She was such a troublesome child that she was sent away to live with her grandfather for the final stretch of Abba's difficult pregnancy with Lizzie, the third daughter and the inspiration for Beth. By contrast, Jo's moods are depicted as charming, her emotional states never so violent that they alienate the reader. Her enthusiasm and excitability never reach the level of out-of-control mania. The one time we are given the opportunity to dislike Jo comes after Amy, in a bratty fit, tosses Jo's writing in the fireplace. We are told it's a book Jo has been working on for years, so it is easy to understand why Jo would be devastated and refuse to talk to her sister. But when a thoroughly ashamed and contrite Amy tries to win Jo's forgiveness, following Jo and Laurie as they go ice-skating, Jo purposefully pretends not to see Amy tagging along behind them and doesn't convey Laurie's warning that the middle of the ice is unsafe for skating. Amy immediately plunges through the ice into the frozen river. Jo and Laurie pull

Amy out and by nightfall, all is fine again. Amy is forgiven. Jo is forgiven.

Nonetheless, after Amy's brush with death, Jo breaks down to Marmee and confesses her fear that she may never be able to cure her temper. "You don't know; you can't guess how bad it is! It seems as if I could do anything when I'm in a passion; I get so savage, I could hurt any one, and enjoy it. I'm afraid I *shall* do something dreadful some day, and spoil my life, and make everybody hate me. Oh, mother! help me, do help me!"

Marmee reassures Jo that they are not unalike; that, in fact, her temper used to be just as bad. "I've been trying to cure it for forty years, and have only succeeded in controlling it. I am angry nearly every day of my life, Jo; but I have learned not to show it; and I still hope to learn not to feel it, though it may take me another forty years to do so."

It reads like a passage from a different book and Jo, rightly so, reacts in utter surprise. Nothing in the chapters preceding suggests Marmee is anything but saintly in her patience and superhuman in her restraint with her children. And no matter how badly things go for the March family, Marmee is always looking out for others who are worse off. Has it all been a tightly managed façade? Is the beauty of womanhood learning to manage one's anger every day of one's life? How is not expressing anger different from repressing it? We never learn exactly what Marmee is angry about, and because of it, as a child, I didn't buy it. I saw it as artifice, an authorial decision to make us think Marmee is the perfect woman—capable of passion and high tempers but never so much that it interferes with her goodness. Real anger is volcanic and active. There is no keeping it down.

My own mother often flew into rages on account of our financial woes, which she sometimes attributed to my father (he was the one, after all, who made the decision to leave China in search of whatever hazy notion of a "better life" was available in America), and other times attributed to dumb, bad luck. Behind the closed doors of our home, my mother bemoaned the state of our lives some nights and other nights swung sharply in the other direction, bursting with unexplained optimism, reiterating to me how everything that had happened thus far in her life had been fortunate. How as a young girl she loved to sing and dance and act and even had producers knocking at her door with promises to make her the next

"Chinese Shirley Temple," but my grandmother refused and sent all the producers and agents away, unwilling to let her daughter fall into the sleazy sex and drug den that was the entertainment world, and rather than feel resentful at my grandmother for denying her the chance to pursue her passions, she was grateful, truly grateful! Or so she said.

Abba Alcott, the real-life matriarch of the Alcott family, was less even-keeled than her fictional counterpart, did not contain her anger as successfully, and was even more tireless and overworked as a result of her husband's repeated failures to provide for the family. While supporting her husband's experimental utopian commune, Fruitlands, which, like all his ventures, eventually failed, Abba wrote in her diary, "There was only one slave at Fruitlands . . . and that was a woman," evincing more than a hint of bitterness. Louisa observed a similar unjust dynamic, that the men of Fruitlands "were so busy discussing and defining great duties that they forgot to perform the small ones." Staying true to one's ideals always comes at a cost, and in the case of the Alcotts, it was often Abba and her daughters who paid it. In another diary entry, Abba wrote, "a woman may live a whole life of sacrifice and at her death meekly say, 'I die a woman.' But a man passes with a few years in experiments in self-denial and simple life, and he says, 'Behold, I am a God.'"

Perhaps Louisa didn't need to detail what Marmee is so angry about nearly every day of her life. To be a woman is to know anger. To be underestimated, treated as inferior, have one's concerns classified as minor, to do all the work and receive none of the glory—how could one *not* feel angry? And yet in order to be a good woman who stands a chance at being loved and accepted, back then and still very much so now, one has to learn, as Marmee advises Jo, not to show it, even better not to *feel* it. Anger in a woman runs the risk of being pathologized, penalized, criminalized. A woman is supposed to bear the violence of patriarchy—both the bloody and the bloodless forms—with unflappable cheeriness.

Why must we learn to control it? I wonder now, no longer the little girl I was back then, who would not stand for my mother's criticism of my father, who considered my mother's capacity for rage an unforgivable defect, who only saw how tirelessly my father worked to give our family a good life, and who dismissed the sacrifices my mother had made, including leaving the only family, friends, and country she had known to move to a foreign land where she did not speak the language and where she would never have the opportunity to advance beyond being someone's assistant or someone's secretary, working full-time while also being a full-time wife and mother, and not only supporting my father in obvious ways but also supporting him emotionally, taking over the duties of staying in touch with family overseas (not just hers but his as well), welcoming my father's parents into her home not once, not twice, but five separate times, each time lasting over a year, all the while managing her own loneliness, isolation, culture shock, and depression. How could I blame her for bouncing between having faith in the world and sinking into inconsolable despair? How could I blame her for lashing out? As an adult, I see now we are hardest on the people who mirror the shadowy parts of ourselves, the parts we don't want to see.

My mother's anger was far more visible than Marmee's, but like Marmee, she did not want me to show anger—it was not feminine and I had not yet secured a husband, which made it even more imperative that

I keep my passions in check. She kept hers contained at home. No friend, acquaintance, coworker, or family member outside of our nuclear unit could ever have guessed that my mother had a temper. Like Marmee, she was an angel to everyone who encountered her—generous and beneficent, always the first to extend a helping hand, always ready to open up our home to anyone who needed a hot meal and a place to stay. Other people confided their sorrows to her and she always knew exactly what kind of consolation to offer in return, keeping her own miseries hidden. My father and I were the only ones who ever saw her complain.

And so my mother, despite her own voluptuous rage, had little patience for mine. Like my mother, I could turn on a dime, go from pure giddiness to utter sorrow to rage blackout to numbed-out depression in an instant. The key difference between us was that I was covetous in addition to rageful. *Some people get everything while I get nothing* was my constant refrain, all my journal entries circled around it, it was the thrum in my brain that never turned off, the *why meeeee* pity party no one could argue me out of. The more I sulked in my despair, the more vividly I imagined other people's good fortune. Like Jo,

I would grumble that other people have all the fun while "I have all the work. It isn't fair, oh, it isn't fair!" When Jo's bad behavior costs her a trip to Paris that her sister Amy is granted instead, Jo predicts Amy is destined to have a charmed, easy life even if becoming an artist doesn't pan out for her. "'You'll marry some rich man, and come home to sit in the lap of luxury all your days,' said Jo." When Amy protests that, if she can't be an artist, she would devote herself to the goodliness of philanthropic work, Jo doesn't believe it. "'Hum!' said Jo, with a sigh; 'if you wish it you'll have it, for your wishes are always granted—mine never.'"

"An old maid—that's what I'm to be."

As it turns out, Amy definitively does not possess the gift of genius in her art; unlike Jo, she is merely talented. As it also turns out, in the world of *Little Women* genius does not guarantee happiness; if anything, it creates a fortress of solitude around the genius herself. Jo's prediction for Amy comes true—she is given the most storybook ending of all the March sisters. She gets to travel through England and France, hobnobbing in fine society, and then spends approximately two paragraphs mourning Beth's death before she is swept into a dazzling love affair with Laurie, who is still massively loaded and no longer pining for Jo. The two marry while abroad and return home radiantly in love.

> Amy's face was full of the soft brightness which betokens a peaceful heart, her voice had a new tenderness in it, and the cool, prim carriage was changed to a gentle dignity, both womanly and winning. No little affectations marred it, and the cordial sweetness of her manner was more charming than the new beauty or the old grace, for it stamped her at once with the unmistakable sign of the true gentlewoman she had hoped to become.

Essentially: Amy's got a man and everything about her is improved! Marmee remarks of Amy, "Love has done much for our little girl," which begs the question: What has the *lack* of romantic love done for our heroine Jo, now approaching her twenty-fifth birthday?

After rejecting Laurie's declaration of love and running off to New York to serve as a governess and get away from it all, only to come back to find out her beloved Beth is dying, Jo finally submits to the cult of true womanhood. This late attempt at mastering feminine devotion and domestic goddessness, however, is of no use. Beth dies a beatific death anyway, and suddenly the book shifts—it is no longer about the four March sisters, but two married women and a soon-to-be spinster with no prospects. In a chapter pointedly titled "All Alone," Alcott fills us in on Jo's state of mind in the months after Beth's death:

> She tried in a blind, hopeless way to do her duty, secretly rebelling against it all the while, for it seemed unjust that her few joys should be lessened, her burdens made heavier, and life get harder and harder as she toiled along. Some people seemed to get all the sunshine, and some all shadow; it was not fair, for she tried more than Amy to be good, but never got any reward,—only disappointment, trouble, and hard work.
>
> Poor Jo! these were the dark days to her, for something like despair came over her when she thought of spending all her life in that quiet house, devoted to humdrum cares, a few poor little pleasures, and the duty that never seemed to grow any easier. "I can't do it. I wasn't meant

for a life like this, and I know I shall break away and do something desperate if somebody don't come and help me," she said to herself, when her first efforts failed, and she fell into the moody, miserable state of mind which often comes when strong wills have to yield to the inevitable.

What was the inevitable, exactly? That no woman can surpass the limits of her gender or her class? That even the most radical amongst us must eventually cave to the hellish prison that is the capitalist cis-hetero patriarchy, or else be punished for trying to resist? We never find out because by the end of the book Jo is married to the slovenly-dressed, uninspiring, much older Professor Bhaer and gives up writing in order to start a school for boys. Though we start the book with Jo wanting to be a boy, the gender binary is in full force by the end of the book—girls must grow up into selfless, sacrificing women, while boys may do as they wish, under the care, wisdom, and worship of the women who feed, clothe, motivate, and care for them.

Perhaps what I objected to most about Jo is how she starts off so ahead of her three sisters—showing gender-queer bravado and resisting conventionality—but by the end of the book, she seems the furthest behind, even more childish and stunted than Beth, who dies a selfless saint and is immortalized as a girl who never got to be a woman. Jo clings to her identity as a "daughter" and "sister" long after her own sisters have downgraded those to mere tertiary categories behind "wife" and "mother." Jo's self-pep talk is more than a touch strained as she tries to talk herself into being at peace with her fate:

> "An old maid—that's what I'm to be. A literary spinster, with a pen for a spouse, a family of stories for children, and twenty years hence a morsel of fame, perhaps; when, like poor Johnson, I'm old, and can't enjoy it—solitary, and can't share it, independent, and don't need it. Well, I needn't be a sour saint nor a selfish sinner; and, I dare say, old maids are very comfortable when they get used to it; but—" and there Jo sighed, as if the prospect was not inviting.

In rare direct address, the narrator of *Little Women* interjects to let us know the state of the union for young women of a certain class in post–Civil War America:

Thirty seems the end of all things to five-and-twenty; but it's not so bad as it looks, and one can get on quite happily if one has something in one's self to fall back upon. At twenty-five, girls begin to talk about being old maids, but secretly resolve that they never will; at thirty, they say nothing about it, but quietly accept the fact; and, if sensible, console themselves by remembering that they have twenty more useful, happy years, in which they may be learning to grow old gracefully. Don't laugh at the spinsters, dear girls, for often very tender, tragical romances are hidden away in the hearts that beat so quietly under the sober gowns, and many silent sacrifices of youth, health, ambition, love itself, make the faded faces beautiful in God's sight. Even the sad, sour sisters should be kindly dealt with, because they have missed the sweetest part of life if for no other reason; and, looking at them with compassion, not contempt, girls in their bloom should remember that they too may miss the blossom time—that rosy cheeks don't last forever, that silver threads will come into the bonnie brown hair, and that

by and by, kindness and respect will be as sweet
as love and admiration now.

It's a much softer version of a speech I had been hearing
long before I even hit puberty. Ever since I could remember, my parents warned me against spinsterhood. To be
born a girl and never grow up to be someone's mother,
well that, my mother used to tell me in Chinese, is the
most tragic existence possible. Worse than tragic, she'd
often add. It means her time on earth was for nothing.

She may as well not have been born? I suggested once,
thinking if I could show my mother how dramatic she
sounded, she might back off, but it only galvanized her.

Yes, she said gravely. A girl who never marries and
never has children is no one at all. She may as well have
never existed.

Once when I was still in grade school, my father took
me with him to visit two women, sisters he knew from
Shanghai, who now lived together in a big three-story
house in the suburbs of Long Island. One of them was
unmarried and the other had a husband, but only on
paper, as he was always away on some business trip. The
visit was meant to be a teachable moment, because these
sisters had it all—money, nice clothing, gourmet food,

fancy cars—but they didn't have a man around to open up a bottle of orange juice.

Can you believe it? my parents said to me. To live in a house like that and not even be able to drink the juice you bought from the supermarket! Your father has to go once every two weeks, my mother said, to open all the jars for them.

That was my first warning. Not long after, during a trip back to China, my parents introduced me to a distant aunt who was not only a spinster but apparently completely out of her mind. I had been told when she was young she was stunning, and knew it. Vanity, excessive belief in one's own self-worth, was a cardinal sin for any woman. My aunt had basked too much in her own looks, enjoyed too much the attention from men, and flaunted her beauty, jumping from man to man, always looking for someone better, richer, more handsome, more romantic, more devoted, until one day she was too old for any man, and there was suddenly no one left to jump into a relationship with. So she had a mental breakdown. She had run out the clock with her greed, with her belief that she was too good for anyone, and ended up with nothing.

I didn't quite believe all this, perhaps because I hadn't

even fully hit puberty yet and it was hard to imagine myself as a shrill old hag with nothing ahead of me but a possible stint in a mental institution. What was so dangerous about desire? Why was there a time limit for women? Why was it so wrong to believe in oneself? Why did we have to follow the rules of settling down (which to me might as well have been a synonym for "settling for") by a certain age or be sentenced to eternal damnation? Men, like Bronson Alcott, seemed to have carte blanche to undertake one grand failed experiment after another, all their adventures and freedom to believe in themselves underwritten by a patriarchal structure that rewarded the delusional, outsized egos of men and punished any woman who dared to think herself capable of greatness. Women had to live for others while men got to live for themselves. Why was it that there was nothing worse than dying alone for a woman, whereas for a man, there was nothing worse than to die forgotten? Being egotistical about having genius and daring might be lauded in a man, but for a woman, it's considered indulgent and immature.

The confusing part about these early lessons in avoiding spinsterhood was how they coincided and clashed so thoroughly with equally urgent lessons against *ever* acting on any kind of sexual desire. A young girl had to remain innocent. Even to have desires of the flesh was unthinkable, it was certain death, a clear path to utter self-destruction, the end of any kind of future worth living. The constant clamor of different alarm bells ringing in locked opposition with each other made rebellion confusing. Rejecting one thing sometimes meant inadvertently agreeing with another. I was supposed to be an aggressive prude who would rather kill a man with my bare hands than let one touch me, but if I wasn't engaged to a man within twenty-four hours after graduating college, a man who wanted to put a baby in me within the first six months of marriage, then I was in danger of becoming a useless washed-up rag. Everything, apparently, had to be timed perfectly, or else, death!

For my atheist Chinese mother who immigrated to the U.S. in her early thirties, staying a virgin until marriage wasn't about not sinning or remaining virtuous, and to whatever extent her warnings could be considered slut-shaming, they were a variety that seemed cartoonishly childish, like rejecting a kiss from a boy on the playground because he has *cooties*, or because *boys are gross.* My mother was always open about how much she loved being a daughter and tried to stay one as long as possible. At times it sounded like she got married only to please my grandmother. For my mother, it was utterly unfathomable that a girl might want to be touched by anyone outside of her own family in any way that was beyond the physical affection that a shared bloodline permitted—how could such a thought even exist? She loved to tell me how even into her twenties, she knew and cared so little about sex that she thought a woman could get pregnant just by sitting too close to a man. I was terrified to let your father even hold my hand, she would tell me.

My parents had emigrated from China a couple years before me, and once they finally got everything in order for me to join them in New York, there was the question of who would take me. I knew nothing of the world except the ten-block radius in Shanghai that included my two sets of grandparents' homes, my preschool, and the meat and vegetable market where we bought our daily groceries. Eventually it was decided that a family friend I had no recollection of ever meeting would take me, as he was planning to go to New York around the same time. This grown man and complete stranger held my hand and walked me through the boarding gate, down the aisle of the plane to our seats, and covered me with a blanket when I tired myself so much from sobbing that I abruptly fell asleep. He held my hand as we switched planes in Anchorage. He led me, by hand, to my parents when we finally landed in New York. I had been delivered to them by a man essentially hired to look after me. Like a debutante, I was ushered out into a new echelon of society. I was four and a half years old and I felt like my innocent days of being a carefree child were already behind me.

I didn't know anything about men or sex, my mother told me over and over again; on her wedding night, she said, all she wanted to do was go home to her parents' house. And because my father was a softie who didn't want to see my mother cry on their wedding night, he agreed that they should spend the first night of their married life, not in their new home as husband and wife, but in my mother's childhood home where she was still her mother's daughter.

"I *am* lonely, sometimes, but I dare say it's good for me."

Part two of *Little Women* is punctuated with a deeper flavor of misery than part one. Jo is utterly betrayed when she finds out Meg loves Laurie's tutor, the humble and devoted John Brooke, who is as exciting as a saltine cracker and is therefore perfect for Meg, who always did aspire to very achievable goals in life. The breakup of the March family is more devastating and real to Jo than the possibility of a future where she might start her own. Louisa herself never married, and she remained steadfastly a daughter from the day she was born until the day she died. When the editor Thomas Niles asked Louisa to write a book for girls, she scoffed at the idea but eventually agreed to do it on the condition that he publish her father as well, who had written a book no one wanted. And so *Little Women* was written not purely out of self-interest; it was, at least partially, motivated by daughterly devotion and a desire to help her father.

After her father suffered a series of debilitating strokes in 1888, Louisa went to visit him and he reportedly told her, "I am going up. Come with me." A day later, Louisa herself fell into a coma, perhaps finally succumbing to the slow burn of mercury poisoning from calomel she took for the typhoid fever she had contracted some twenty years earlier while nursing Union soldiers during the Civil War, and died two days after her father. She was reportedly buried at the foot of her parents' and her sister Lizzie's graves—devoted daughter and sister until the end.

In the book, when the business of Meg and John Brooke sitting in a tree is made known to Jo, she laments, "I just wish I could marry Meg myself, and keep her safe in the family." The deep attachment to family turns incestuous when one cannot age appropriately out of it. As a child, I was ashamed of Jo for not wanting to grow up, for wanting everything to stay as it had always been. My mother would often express to me her desire for time to stop, so I could be her baby forever. I was on the fence. I wanted to grow up even as I feared it. I had slept in the same bed as my parents the first two and a half years of my life. My father recalled waking up every hour in the first year to make sure neither he nor my mother rolled over and accidentally crushed me in their sleep. When I immigrated to America, I continued to sleep in the same bed as my parents. The closeness we shared was in part cultural—it's much more accepted and encouraged in Chinese society for children to share a bed with their parents late into childhood. Based on anecdotal evidence, at least half of the Chinese mothers

I knew shared a bed with their daughters until they went off to college, while the fathers slept in separate beds. For immigrants, this closeness can also be chalked up to lack of resources. I grew up sharing a house with several families, and the idea of having a separate bed, never mind separate bedrooms, was a luxury we could not afford in our first years in America. So when our economic situation improved, when we moved out of the first few neighborhoods where we lived, when we got a three-bedroom house in the suburbs with a garage and driveway, a living room *and* a den, an eat-in kitchen *and* a dining room, a front yard *and* a backyard, I began to see my mother's physical affection for me as inappropriate. Now that we had all of this space, why on earth would I still crawl into her bed and let her spoon me? I was growing up and I wanted to be everything my parents feared.

Or perhaps my parents lost me the moment I landed in America. I had been ripped away from my extended family and the home I had known, plopped into a foreign land to be reunited with parents I no longer remembered, and forced to start kindergarten not knowing any English words except "bathroom," "yes," and "no." On the first day of school, a boy in my class who had been left back twice emerged out of nowhere and saved me. Every day, he would take my hand when the last bell rang and personally escort me through a throng of would-be bullies and tormentors, and not let go of my hand until he had personally transferred it from his to my mother's, just as that strange man had held my hand above the clouds and across the Pacific Ocean to lead me to my mother earlier that summer. Was that when I began to eroticize men as saviors? Was that why I despised Jo from the moment she appears on the page? Because she desires to be as free as a man rather than to be saved by one?

Jo is so difficult to pin down and capture that no matter how many times he tries, Laurie discovers he can't write Jo into his breakup opera:

> He wanted Jo for his heroine, and called upon his memory to supply him with tender recollections and romantic visions of his love. But memory turned traitor; and, as if possessed by the perverse spirit of the girl, would only recall Jo's oddities, faults, and freaks, would only show her in the most unsentimental aspects,—beating mats

with her head tied up in a bandanna, barricading herself with the sofa-pillow, or throwing cold water over his passion *à la* Gummidge,—and an irresistible laugh spoilt the pensive picture he was endeavoring to paint. Jo wouldn't be put into the Opera at any price, and he had to give her up.

It was impossible to turn her into an object. She was always the protagonist of her own story; no man was up to the task of writing her into his.

Let a man take care of you, be less strong, that's how a woman should be, my mother warned me a few years ago. Don't try so hard to be special, just be *normal*. You'll see, she said. You'll see how hard it is to be strong on your own. But I knew already, I felt it every time someone told me I was strong, or intimidating, or different. Sometimes it felt amazing and other times it was deadening. I felt the sting of being "strong" when I was asked to write about Jo March for this book. Out of all the March sisters, Jo? Why was I suited to write about Jo and not basic-ass Meg who gets everything she wants and plays by the rules? Why not spoiled little Amy who is literally saved by Laurie over and over again, offered a free trip to Europe, and comes back married and financially secure for the rest of her life? Why not angelic Beth who is nothing but dutiful and good and rewarded with early death, so selfless and allergic to taking up space that the mourning of her death isn't even awarded a full chapter? Why did it fall on me to write about Jo?

I thought I was feminine like Meg, fragile like Beth, and vain like Amy. I thought I needed love, companionship, and touch just like everyone else. At times I have needed help more than I have needed people to see me as self-sufficient. And yet, like Jo in part one of *Little Women*, I doggedly pursued writing and some elusive, stupid notion of "genius" more than I pursued whatever notions of domestic bliss my parents and mainstream society tried to program me and every other little girl into wanting. Maybe I committed the same sin my spinster aunt and all the spinsters before me committed— thought I could have it all when, in reality, all women must choose. When it came down to choosing a romantic relationship or writing, I always chose writing. I wanted to devote myself to writing books more than I wanted to devote myself to a man. Was that a false dichotomy? I don't know.

Of course a girl can grow up into a woman and hold multiple identities—daughter, sister, mother, wife, friend, comrade, artist, writer, iconoclast, leader—but without being a "wife" and especially without being a "mother," one's womanhood is called into question. To pursue art at the cost of starting a family, to not have it all, but to just have one—a career and not a family—is seen as brave, but tragic. Having reached my mid-thirties without a ring or a baby bump in sight, I have started to resent when other people, especially those who are married with children, praise me for not caving into societal pressures. Equally irritating is to be the recipient of other people's pity.

When Laurie and Amy come home from Europe, Laurie finds his old friend Jo hiding behind a pillow and comments on how terribly she's aged, how sad she looks. Jo, for her part, refuses to play the role of the poor spinster.

> "You *are* older; here's a line, and there's another; unless you smile, your eyes look sad, and when I touched the cushion, just now, I found a tear on it. You've had a great deal to bear, and had to bear it alone . . ."

But Jo only turned over the traitorous pillow, and answered in a tone which she tried to make quite cheerful,—

"No, I had father and mother to help me, the dear babies to comfort me, and the thought that you and Amy were safe and happy, to make the troubles here easier to bear. I *am* lonely, sometimes, but I dare say it's good for me."

Near the end of *Little Women*, Jo is miserable and alone. It may be well and good to decide, as Jo has several times throughout the book, "I don't believe I shall ever marry; I'm happy as I am, and love my liberty too well to be in any hurry to give it up for any mortal man," but when nearly everyone you love is a woman who *has* decided to marry and give up their liberty for mere mortal men, you are left all alone to bear the consequence of your decision to live for yourself. Like Jo, I *am* lonely sometimes, but I don't need to convince myself it's good for me. I may not be able to (or want to) alter my entire way of thinking in order to rescue myself from loneliness, but that doesn't mean I enjoy it either. Maybe I am rebelling now against the idea that I might be any kind of rebel. My life has not been in the service of some kind of resistance or in accordance with any great ideology. I don't wish to be twisted into a lesson for some young girl one day, either as an example to emulate or one to avoid at all costs. I don't need to write yet another rallying cry against the oppressiveness of convention, or a bitter treatise on how I should have chosen a more orthodox existence. I don't wish to be idealized or scorned. Sometimes I just want to shed a tear in peace, without it being a statement about anything at all.

"I'm the one that will have to fight and work, and climb and wait, and maybe never get in after all."

In part one of the book, when the sisters are still little women, Jo (who as self-declared "man of the house" is more of a probationary little woman than the rest) muses while they hike to their secret spot where they go for a glimpse of heaven, "Wouldn't it be fun if all the castles in the air which we make could come true, and we could live in them?" When Beth expresses concern she may not be good enough to make it to the good place, whatever that may be, Jo reassures her, "You'll get there, Beth, sooner or later; no fear of that," and then adds a self-pitying coda, "I'm the one that will have to fight and work, and climb and wait, and maybe never get in after all."

Ten years later, in the very last chapter of the book, the three married sisters revisit their castles. Meg assesses that hers is the most realized: "I asked for splendid things, to be sure, but in my heart I knew I should be satisfied, if I had a little home, and John, and some dear children like these. I've got them all, thank God, and am the happiest woman in the world." Amy too is happy with how her castle has turned out, even though it is different from what she envisioned as a child. "I don't relinquish all my artistic hopes, or confine myself to helping others fulfil their dreams of beauty. I've begun to model a figure of baby, and Laurie says it is the best thing I've ever done." The ghost of Beth does not get a say, but for me, the most disturbing part is how Jo, now married and rechristened Mrs. Bhaer, remarks, as if under hypnosis, that her original castle was too "selfish, lonely and cold . . . I haven't given up the hope that I may write a good book yet, but I can wait, and I'm sure it will be all the better for such experiences and illustrations as these," referring to her sons.

The many young girls who were fans of part one of

Little Women wrote to Louisa in droves, insisting that Jo and Laurie were endgame. But Louisa refused to give her readers exactly what they wanted. Nonetheless, she did yield to the pressures put on her by her publisher and by devotees of *Little Women*, despite her original plan to keep Jo a literary spinster. In the 150 years since the novel's publication, readers' responses to Jo's marriage to Professor Bhaer have been varied—some view it as cheekily feminist while for others, it's totally disappointing. But one thing is to be said—Jo *chooses* Bhaer. She is the one who stoops down to kiss him, a traditionally masculine gesture. She leads him into her home, and he follows. She's the domme, he's the sub, at least in that moment. A chapter later, she becomes a wife and gives up writing. I've often wondered whether Jo would still be quite so beloved, if Louisa had written her closer to her actual life.

When I was exactly Jo's age at the start of the book—fifteen—I had a small brass bell on my dresser table. No idea where it came from, but it opened up and was hollow inside. I anointed it the keeper of my future dreams—not quite a castle in the sky, but a bell in my room, anyway. I wrote on a piece of paper *I want someone to love me*, folded it up, and kept it inside the bell. It was my only wish. I didn't think to jot down anything about my writing. One, after all, was a wish, and the other was something I could actually work toward, something I could earn with some determination and grit. Love, on the other hand, was not in my hands, it was in the hands of fate. It was something one prayed for, not worked for.

Years later, as I was editing my first book of fiction, I enlisted my parents to help translate a famous Chinese folk song, "Fairy Couple Returning Home," for one of the stories where the mother sings karaoke to relive her glory days in China and to connect with the singer she could have been if only her life hadn't been wrecked by the Cultural Revolution and then again by her husband's decision to come to America. I remember my parents singing that song together many times, in particular on their twenty-fifth anniversary. I sat on the couch in the family room of our split-level Long Island house and watched as my parents sang the song to me.

You hear this song a lot at weddings, my father told me.

One day your daddy and I will sing it at your wedding, my mother added, and on that occasion, it touched me.

I saw what they were so afraid of, but even more I

saw what they were looking forward to. It wasn't only about how my decaying, rotting body had been created for nothing if I wasn't someone's wife and someone's mother, but also about how ceremony imparts meaning to the people participating in it. Our lives as immigrants in America were bereft of ceremony; the culture my parents came from had no home in America, and so it died a little bit each day. The rituals that most people organize their lives around, the milestones that we celebrate within a community—all of that had been axed out of my parents' lives. We were atheists, big neutralized nothings. Maybe, I thought, in regard to their lifelong mission to get me married, all they wanted was a ceremony and the magic that comes with it.

During the time my parents helped me with the translation, I learned that the song comes from an old Chinese folk opera that has undergone many revisions and interpretations. With each passing era, the work warps a little more, becoming what people need it to become. It was originally a folktale about a fairy goddess who goes down to earth in search of her lost weaving equipment and coat of feathers, which she needs to fly. While on earth, she falls in love with a mortal man, a struggling peasant who has sold himself into indentured servitude to pay for his father's funeral. The song is about her choice to give up her immortality in order to be with her lover. They sing about all the struggles they will have to endure, and how they aren't afraid, for when two people in love have each other, even the bitter aspects of life are sweet. During the Communist era, it became a story about proletarian struggle. Nowadays it's back to being a love story—two people from literally two different worlds decide they are better together and will give up anything for each other. In the end the goddess decides to go low rather than fly high.

Once, when I was little, I asked my mother if she regretted not becoming a famous singer, or renowned actress, or acclaimed writer.

No, she replied immediately. Because then I wouldn't have had you.

It was an either/or situation. She could have been a great artist or she could have been a loving wife and mother. In the end, the choice had been made for her, and she was grateful she had a small, happy life of family rather than a big, lonely one of fame.

The weekend before my first book of stories came

out, I went back to my parents' house, the one they had moved to several years before when downsizing and to be closer to the city. My parents had lovingly recreated my teenage bedroom, given me a whole room in their new house even though I was no longer their little girl, although maybe according to traditional Chinese culture, I still was, because I was unmarried, and so I remained stunted in girlhood. I rarely stayed in that bedroom and treated it as a storage container that I would occasionally rifle through. On this visit, I found the brass bell I had used to store my most secret desire, my castle in the air, opened it up, and found nothing inside. My parents must have found the note during the move and thrown it away.

I was finally the writer I always wanted to be; still, I was melancholy. I felt like Jo March in the third act of *Little Women*, wondering if she had made a mistake all those years ago. Did she reject the wrong things, the wrong people? Her creator interjects to ask us, and perhaps also to ask herself, "Was it all self-pity, loneliness, or low spirits? or was it the waking up of a sentiment which had bided its time as patiently as its inspirer? Who shall say." Really, who can say?

CARMEN MARIA MACHADO ON BETH

A DEAR AND NOTHING ELSE

"The big house did prove a Palace Beautiful, though it took some time for all to get in, and Beth found it very hard to pass the lions."

I WAS SICK a lot as a kid, though I don't know if you'd call me sickly. I wouldn't have called myself sickly. I didn't have a *sick bed*. I wasn't sent to the seashore for the bracing salt air or the desert for its aridity. I didn't convalesce. I watched the film version of *The Secret Garden* and scoffed at Colin, that little pale comma of a boy in a boat of a bed who was only sick because no one had made him *walk* or go *outside*, not realizing the demented dimensions of my scorn.

Many of my symptoms—abdominal pain, nausea and vomiting, assorted gastrointestinal complaints—have stayed with me into adulthood. Some have been partially explained, some have not; I manage them as best I can. I don't have to go to doctors with the same frequency as I did in the past. When I think about my body's enduring vices and mysteries too hard, it makes me anxious. If my life were a novel, I would worry about my character, wondering if my premature death is written on the wall.

The symptoms were severe enough that my parents spent several years taking me to specialists to locate a source, which they never really did. I did my best to torment the doctors, and my mother, at every turn. I did not go to my appointments willingly, and more than once my mother dragged me out from underneath my bed in order to get me to the doctor's office. I did not obediently stick out my arm so that they, vampires, could take my blood. My mother offered to take me to Waldenbooks—then B. Dalton, then Borders, as the chains multiplied and vanished in turn—if I was good. I could get one book, I could get two or three, I could get the new Animorphs books *and* frozen yogurt from TCBY *and* she'd let me stay home from school. Sometimes the bribes worked, sometimes they didn't. They ran up against our respective worst traits: my fear and stubbornness, my mother's intractable resentment and umbrage at having to bribe me at all. Often, we ended up going home and sitting in silence in front of *All My Children* while she ironed; to this day, the smell of clothes being pressed makes me think of Susan Lucci's swooping, oversized bangs.

During one particularly bad appointment, I pulled my arms inside of my sweatshirt and knotted them against my torso. This story has been retold many times within my family with increasing hyperbole—my sister once told someone "six fat nurses had to hold her down," even though she was only five when it happened and wasn't even there—but the way I remember it, a nurse grabbed each arm, my mother grabbed my squirming lower half, and someone else drew the blood while I screamed the kind of scream that, in a horror movie, would indicate a demon leaving my body.

I was not a good sick kid. I catastrophized. I howled. I refused the bribery, and then demanded it. I kicked and hit. I sobbed and, when I learned how, swore. I told my mother I hated her. I told the medical professionals I'd rather do anything than have one more doctor touch me. I told them I'd rather die.

When I was seven—before the symptoms manifested themselves, but when I was already a weirdo and a nervous wreck—I read *Little Women* for the first time. The book was a gift from my godmother, Eleanor Jacobs. In her twenties, my mother had worked for Eleanor as a personal assistant and aide. When I was a kid, Eleanor was in her eighties and in an assisted living facility because she had multiple sclerosis.

Though I didn't know it yet, Eleanor was a woman after my own heart. Her late husband had worked as a distributor for Paramount, though she'd been widowed since the sixties, and she had spent many years living in Guatemala, Trinidad, Panama. Eleanor was the epitome of elegance and worldliness, a formidable woman who, when she died, was only two days shy of her ninety-sixth birthday. She had a deep and raspy voice—a smoker's voice, though I don't know if she smoked; when they flew, my mother would show up to the airport in sweatpants and Eleanor in white gloves and full makeup and with all her jewelry on because you always needed to look your best to fly.

Every summer, when we visited my mother's people in Wisconsin, we made a special trek to Madison to visit Eleanor. I loved her long-term care facility. It was like a mini-city, a single building with everything one might need. On the way to Eleanor's room from the entrance, we would walk past endless open doors; you could see, in turn, women having their hair pressed, a group playing pinochle, a resident weaving on a loom. At the intersection between two corridors there was a massive aviary, full of bright and radiant songbirds. In Eleanor's room, we had our ritual: she'd give me a feathery peck on my cheek, which left a bright streak of lipstick behind. Then, she'd gesture to the corner, where the nurses had artfully arranged my gifts.

While she occasionally gave me a little something else—a personalized stationery set, journals, newspaper clippings about powerful women or writers, once, a silver locket—Eleanor primarily gifted me books. She had a distinctive type: female-centered classic literature—*Little Women*, *The Secret Garden*, *A Little Princess*—and long and difficult works of nonfiction with a decidedly feminist bent: the collected letters of Susan B. Anthony, a book about the first ladies, *The Diary of Anne Frank*. She didn't give presents like that to my siblings, and that led me to conclude that they were not gifts meant to direct me toward new and better literature, not moral instruction manuals or pointed prescriptions for good behavior. Instead, these gifts were intended to draw out something deep inside me, something special, that was already there; something my mother could not sense, but that Eleanor could.

Every time we visited, my mother received no-nonsense marriage advice from Eleanor while I curled up in the corner, reading whatever she'd given me. Every so often, Eleanor would turn to me to ask me questions. How was school? What had I read lately? What was I writing about? They were way more interesting than the questions most adults asked me, about how good I was or how carefully I listened to my parents. They were the kind I wanted to answer.

Little Women impressed the hell out of me. It was, as a physical object, beautiful and distinctly dangerous. It was also huge, the hugest book I'd ever seen. It seemed to have its own gravity, to pull other books around it on the shelf into its formidable orbit. I liked carrying it around because it impressed and confused adults, which was at that age my primary concern. One of my teachers didn't believe I'd read it—as if it were a copy of *War and Peace*—and quizzed me on its plot until she was satisfied.

And it was—I realized upon beginning to read it—very *old*. Not the edition itself, which was new, but the book had been written even before I or my mother or even Eleanor was born. I was still learning what it meant to read "old" books; how they read differently than "new" books. I knew that people wrote books in the past but assumed that they would be impossible to grasp, and yet when I made my way through Alcott's prose I found the story funny and recognizable. I also adored the way the novel resembled Eleanor's home, a little city with so many delightful rooms. Picaresque— or, at the very least, episodic—with magnificent chapter titles like "Amy's Valley of Humiliation," it became a touchstone for me. When people asked me about my favorite books, the list was constantly in flux, but *Little Women* was always there.

I was in a production of *Little Women* in middle school, as Marmee; it was the closest I ever came to a leading role. I got to wear a wonderful red dress. My longtime crush played Mr. March, and when he returned home from war, I was instructed to rush at him and receive a kiss on the cheek. During the scene in which Marmee receives a letter that her husband is gravely ill, I was permitted to clasp my hand to my bosom and swoon into an overstuffed chair.

Revisiting *Little Women*'s little women as an adult was both strange and surprising. Despite my powerful abiding aversion to Amy—her burning of Jo's manuscript created a deep, lifelong terror of losing the only copy of one's words—I have softened toward her a smidge, if only because she changes the most over the course of the novel, while also remaining utterly herself. (Though I still firmly believe that the otherwise very morally pure and instructive plot point of Jo rescuing her when she falls through thin ice and then reflecting guiltily on her own anger would have been far more interesting—and satisfying—if Jo had simply watched her go under.) I am unnerved, as an adult, to identify with Meg the most— that is to say, a boring homebody who wants fine things ("If only I had a silk!"). Jo is of course a delight insofar as she is a writer of infinite invention and imagination who frequently loses herself in her work, but she reads as a bit more tedious—a bit more Mary-Sue, perhaps—to my present self.[1]

1. Far more interesting, and what went over my head as a kid, was Jo's delightful genderfuckery, her queerness. "I'm the man of the family now papa is away," she says in an early chapter, and continues asserting her own masculinity throughout the novel. As a child, I thought that Laurie—prone to "Byronic fits of gloom," a "glorious

But Beth? What was there to say about Beth? Reading the book with her death in mind was singularly odd. I waited for it, like a guillotine. I remembered so little about her that I was surprised to discover that she's alive for a full 80 percent of it. If you'd asked me before the reread, I would have sworn she died somewhere toward the middle, maybe even earlier.

Little Women was an early example of character archetypes as clearly mappable, *Cosmo* magazine–style personality types,[2] a prototype for Harry Potter's houses or *His Dark Materials*' daemons. Are you Jo, the Gryffindor of the group—brave, who suffers no fools while also being insufferable, thinks quite highly of herself, the

---

human boy" who "frolicked and flirted, grew dandified, aquatic, sentimental, [and] gymnastic," "hinted darkly at one all-absorbing passion"— was Jo's *one true love*, and was of course heartbroken when she rejected him. As an adult—and recognizing Jo for who she was—I realized that my heartbreak was an unsettling precognition that they would have made a mercurial but otherwise fine gay couple.

2. As a kid, I played a reissued version of the 1960s Barbie Queen of the Prom board game in which you vied against other players for four distinct dresses, dates, etc. with a clearly designed order of desirability. (Ken, for example, sat on one end, and indicated that in some way or another you'd won; getting Poindexter was a sign that you'd made some terrible choices.)

author-insert character everyone wants to be? Or maybe you're Amy—power-hungry, silly, vain; Slytherin, obviously—Jo's main antagonist within the family. Perhaps Meg, Ravenclaw—dull in personality but smart and interested in the finer things in life. Or maybe—heavens forfend!—you're Hufflepuff Beth: pure and loyal, dowdy and dead.

It is a curious thing, the archetype—a feature of some genres (fairy tale, satire) and a taboo in others (realism). When they appear where they are not expected, they feel curiously incomplete, as if a single character has been lopped apart. But in real life, we love to be shoved into these boxes.[3] We love horoscopes and Myers-Briggs and hometown clichés and other clannish taxidermies.[4] This instinct to put things in easily identifiable categories starts young; it is literally part of childhood development. (Even the aggravating focus on "girl" things and "boy" things is a combination of unnecessary adult

---

3. For the record, I think I'm a Ravenclaw-Meg-Cancer with Slytherin-Jo-Poindexter rising and my daemon is an otter and my otter's daemon is a naked mole rat.

4. More than once, I've been advertised a personalized sweatshirt that reads: "It's a Machado thing, you wouldn't get it."

obsession with gender binaries and children's natural instincts to make things fit into one place or another.) This preoccupation lasts into adulthood for all of the obvious reasons: the desire to be part of a group, comfort in the idea that there are others like you, the latent belief that your personality is, in a way, outside of your control. It also provides a soothing lack of wholeness: the idea that the puzzle-piece that is us is meant to link up with the puzzle-pieces of other people. ("Beth is my conscience," Jo tells Laurie.) It is also a way of defining who we are not: I am not a Slytherin, I am the opposite of a Taurus, I'd rather die than be a Meg. Even though, like astrological signs and Hogwarts houses, these qualities only add together to create one, maybe one-and-a-half distinct people, we crave their guidance. We gain much by blunting ourselves against the archetype's hard surface.

Beth is the too-pure-for-this-world archetype made manifest. She is beautiful but sexless, artistic but very embarrassed about it, and it's good that she doesn't demonstrate any kind of ambition[5] because she's going

5. "'We're an ambitious set, aren't we? Every one of us, but Beth, wants to be rich and famous, and gorgeous in every respect. I do

to die. And I don't mean that in a "we're all mortal" sense; she is created with her premature death already seared into the timeline, a fact of her personality. She is born a ghost.

In the first chapter of *Little Women*, when Louisa May Alcott is doling out archetypes to the siblings, Beth asks, "If Jo is a tomboy and Amy a goose, what am I, please?"

"You're a dear," Meg answers, "and nothing else."

People who have studied anything about *Little Women* know that the novel is based, roughly, on Louisa's family, a clan of thinkers, artists, and transcendentalists who rubbed elbows with some of the premier minds of their time: Ralph Waldo Emerson, Henry David Thoreau, Margaret Fuller.

Beth is no exception; she is based on Alcott's second-youngest sister, Lizzie. Lizzie, like Beth, was stricken with scarlet fever.[6] (During this initial illness, her fam-

---

wonder if any of us will ever get our wishes,' said Laurie, chewing grass like a meditative calf."

6. Unlike the novel, in which Beth gets the illness while helping an impoverished family, the real-life Lizzie likely picked up the illness from mother Abba. Louisa wrote in her journal that Lizzie caught it

ily—vegans[7] and believers in alternative medicine[8]—did not send for a doctor.[9]) Like Beth, she recovered from the illness but, her heart weakened, never regained full

———————————

from "poor children Mother nursed when they fell sick, living over a cellar where pigs have been kept."

7. In 1843, the Alcotts participated in a short-lived experiment they called Fruitlands: a vegan, agrarian, transcendentalist utopia in Harvard, Massachusetts. Like so many American utopian experiments—the Shakers, the Oneida Community—the members were progressive for their era but ultimately so ahead of their time they could not sustain themselves. On the ninety-acre farm, Barry Hankins wrote in *The Second Great Awakening and the Transcendentalists*, the group struggled to survive without the assistance of animal labor or products, and also eschewed coffee, tea, and rice, as well as "carrots, beets, and potatoes . . . because they showed a lower nature by growing downwards."

"Wearing [clothes] incapable of warding off the cold," Hankins wrote, "and undernourished by the extremely ascetic diet, members abandoned the idea as winter ensued." But before the experiment failed, the group celebrated Lizzie's eighth birthday. The group decided to give her an imaginary bouquet of flowers. Charles Lane, cofounder of Fruitlands, offered her a fictional piece of moss—humility. Anna offered a rose—grace. May, a tigerlily—passion. Louisa, a lily of the valley—sweetness. And Abba, a forget-me-not.

8. Bronson Alcott in particular was a follower of Samuel Christian Hahnemann, founder of homeopathic medicine.

9. "Anticipating that Lizzie would soon throw off her illness," writes John Matteson in *Eden's Outcasts: The Story of Louisa May Alcott and*

health. Like Beth, she died tragically young, though not quite as young as her literary counterpart.

But while Beth bore her suffering gladly, with unconscionable cheer and resolution, Lizzie was enraged at the fact of her own mortality. "In *Little Women*," writes Alcott biographer Susan Cheever, "Beth has a quiet, dignified death, a fictional death. Although young Lizzie Alcott was a graceful, quiet woman, she was not so lucky. A twenty-two-year-old whose disease had wasted her body so that she looked like a middle-aged woman, she lashed out at her family and her fate with an anger that she had never before expressed." Louisa and the others caring for Lizzie plied her with morphine, ether, and opium, though eventually they lost any effect they once had on her. "[The] pain," writes Cheever in *American Bloomsbury*, "seemed to drive her mad . . . even on large doses of opium, Lizzie attacked her sisters and asked to be left in peace."

By the end, the fight had gone out of her body. The final words her family could understand were, "Well

---

Her Father, "Bronson put much faith in the fact that she had never tasted animal food."

now, mother, I go, I go. How beautiful everything is tonight," though she "kept up a little inaudible monologue" for a short while after that. When she passed, both Louisa and Abba reported seeing a "light mist rise from the body and float up and vanish in the air."

Lizzie was buried in Sleepy Hollow Cemetery in Concord, Massachusetts, on a patch of land she'd chosen before her death. Thoreau and Emerson served as pallbearers. "Emerson told the officiating minister, who did not know the family well, that Lizzie was a good, unselfish, patient child, who made friends even in death," John Matteson wrote in *Eden's Outcasts*. "Everyone seemed to forget that they were not burying a child but a woman of twenty-two."

I once read a distraught, pearl-clutching editorial in a British newspaper that bemoaned the rise of sick-lit. "While the Twilight series and its imitators are clearly fantasy, these books don't spare any detail of the harsh realities of terminal illness, depression, and death," wrote a blusteringly scandalized woman named Tanith Carey. "Most are also liberally peppered with sex and swearing." She claimed to trace the phenomenon back to *The Lovely Bones*—published in 2002—seeming to not know how old the genre of "young people in bodily peril" really was.

I spent the better part of the nineties devouring sick-lit for young people, as well as adult books—memoirs about illness and medical thrillers alike—that hit similarly dramatic and gruesome notes: *Alex, the Life of a Child* (a father tells the story of his daughter's fight against cystic fibrosis); Richard Preston's *The Hot Zone* (in which viral hemorrhagic fevers turn the human body into quivering puddles of blood pudding[10]); all of the Robin Cook novels.[11]

10. I read *The Hot Zone* in one night, under the blankets with a flashlight. It would have been horrifying enough on its own, but when I finished, I turned the book back over to its cover and noticed the copy beneath the title—"A TERRIFYING TRUE STORY"—and those words scrolled through my brain like ticker tape until the sun crept into the sky.

11. During the pre-op appointment for a diagnostic procedure I had when I was a young teenager, I made a nurse promise that they would *not* deliberately screw up my anesthesia in order to harvest my organs from my still-living body. My concerns stemmed from Cook's 1987 best-selling medical thriller *Coma*, which I'd secreted from a church bazaar without my mother's knowledge.

But the genre's undeniable master is Lurlene McDaniel, who has written dozens of books about teenagers at the mercy of cancer, organ failure, and other "faultless" diseases. "In the nineties, librarians started referring to me as the crying-and-dying lady," she once told a bookstore audience, and indeed, that was precisely what I—a highly sensitive burgeoning hypochondriac with some kind of undiagnosed ailment—wanted from a book. I wanted the emotional catharsis that those books could provide—books with titles like *Six Months to Live, I Want to Live, So Much to Live For, No Time to Cry*—even if I spent the whole time reading them checking my body for the telltale bruises that might indicate I had leukemia, imagining what I'd look like without hair.[12]

12. It should be pointed out that this was more or less the explicit purpose of the novels' symptom scenes; "teen sick-lit's unrelenting diagnostic indexing of characters' symptoms also compels readers to imagine their own bodies as subject to an endless 'body project,' encouraging them to self-examine not only for signs of illness (as many fans of the books report doing) but also for other markers of undesirability or abnormality that might be improved." (Julie Passanante Elman, "Nothing Feels as Real.") It is probably not a coincidence that I more than once imagined that the pesky extra pounds I'd gained during the onset of puberty would be conveniently dealt with via chemotherapy if I was (un)lucky enough to have cancer.

Adulthood did not alleviate any of this specific anxiety, though it did change a bit. Instead of using novels as analogue WebMD, I began to think of myself and my body in narrative terms. A few years back, my parents called to tell me my paternal grandmother and aunt had both been diagnosed with breast cancer. Immediately, my mind went to a pulpy V. C. Andrews novel, *Heaven*, that I'd devoured as a preteen. In it, a villainous stepmother—who chapters earlier had disemboweled the protagonist's hamster in revenge for sleeping with her husband—is felled mid-story by an advanced case of breast cancer, which had been missed because of her preternaturally large chest. I had never before considered my own massive bust as a cause for alarm; but afterward, I began the ritual of feeling up myself in the shower in an attempt to locate that fatal lump that could blossom into death, lifting and tugging and pulling at my breast in front of the mirror. "I can feel the cancer," I said to a friend, and I was certain I could, a kind of pinching deep in the tissue. "You can't," she said. "You absolutely can't." I hyperventilated in the cheery parlor of my grad program's building, my head between my knees. *This could be it, this could be it*, I thought. *This is the part of the novel where I am challenged. The complication. Or maybe . . . or maybe it's the end of the whole damn book and I'm about to die.*[13]

In her academic essay "Nothing Feels as Real," on the implications of the sick-lit subgenre, Julie Passanante Elman asserts that the genre is an inherently political one, in which "compulsory" heteronormativity and able-bodiedness are paramount. The genre's primary characteristic is to rehabilitate the "unruly crip/queer" (like *So Much to Live For*'s Marlee, who refuses to be pleasant or wear a headscarf to conceal her partially bald head; her rehabilitation takes the form of a nineties-teen-romcom makeover, though it does not save her in the end). The end of all this wrangling is what Elman calls the "managed heart" of the reader; a genre that purports to "give teens a dose of reality" instead gives them a "powerful cultural fantasy" of rewards and punishments tied to their presentability and agreeableness. (Consider the elegance of Beth's pallor; the romantic, swooning Victorian softness of her illness.) Instead of acknowledging the capriciousness of illness and death—how they strike

13. The fundamental problem with this psychological mindset is that where you are in the narrative of your life entirely depends upon what sort of author is writing your story. Lurlene McDaniel? Terry Pratchett? Jonathan Franzen?

at random, metastasize without warning, and leave no space for narrative neatness—the cultural acceptability of the narrative is paramount.

This mix of signals properly confused me. In addition to being a sick kid, I—to my mind—was not sick enough. I could not imagine being well, but I also could not imagine dying virtuously. My illness was not attractive or romantic—I was not pale or ethereal or waifish or magnificently bald; my illness did not make me fashionably thin. My symptoms involved shitting and vomiting and stomach cramps. I missed enough school to make my life difficult, but not enough that people wondered where I was. I was a sort-of-sick hypochondriac; it was the worst scenario I could imagine.

Little Women is positively lousy with premonitions of Beth's death. Beth is, in turn, forced to stare down her beloved dead canary, Pip—"who lay dead in the cage with his little claws pathetically extended, as if imploring the food for want of which he had died"—and bury him in a domino box,[14] and to cradle a baby dead from

14. In a surviving diary, ten-year-old Lizzie writes of a classmate

the same scarlet fever that would, years later, kill her. Little cruelties and ironies abound throughout the entire book—everything from strawberries in winter[15] to castles in the sky[16] to animal metaphors[17] seem like odd jokes or else Alcott's subconscious planting her grief on every page. But the grief is, otherwise, a strange and flattening thing; beneath its weight, Beth becomes faultless, angelic, positively uncomplicated. Her ambitions are not squashed by her infirmity, because she has none. Her only imperfection—shyness—seems like a humblebrag, like a job candidate telling an interviewer that her primary flaw is "working too hard."

There is also the extended sequence in which we learn that Beth cares for a group of invalid dolls abandoned by

---

bringing in "a little dead squirrel in a paper coffin." Her response is comically neutral: "[It] gave us something to talk about."

15. Shortly before Beth's death, Jo imagines giving her beloved sister "strawberries in winter"; "strawberry tongue" is a classic symptom of scarlet fever.

16. "'If we are all alive ten years hence, let's meet, and see how many of us have got our wishes, or how much nearer we are then than now,' said Jo, always ready with a plan."

17. Called "Mouse" by her family, Beth loves to play with cats.

her more discerning siblings. She cares for them the way she will be cared for one day.

> Not one whole or handsome one among them, all were outcasts till Beth took them in . . . [she] cherished them all the more tenderly for that very reason, and set up a hospital for infirm dolls. No pins were ever stuck into their cotton vitals, no harsh words or blows were ever given them, no neglect ever saddened the heart of the most repulsive, but all were fed and clothed, nursed and caressed with an affection which never failed. . . . If anyone had known the care lavished on [her dolls], I think it would have touched their hearts, even while they laughed.

Reading it, I thought about the hospital I created with my friend Margaret for our American Girl dolls. With the assistance of her mother, who was a nurse, we constructed EKG machines from paper and cardboard and IVs with Ziploc bags and food dye and diagnosed our dolls—hers a Molly and mine a Girl of Today I called Sara, after the protagonist in *A Little Princess*—with terrible diseases that needed immediate attention. It was as frenetic a scene as Beth's was docile—active, whirring care. We created a large and dramatic backstory in which we were sisters, and the dolls our daughters who had matching undiagnosed ailments.[18] I drew stitches on my doll's stomach and my mother almost had a heart attack. She asked me if I knew how expensive the doll had been; I told her mysterious illnesses did not make such judgments.

Within minutes of Lizzie's birth, Bronson Alcott began writing what would eventually be a five hundred-page unpublished[19] manuscript: *Psyche, or the Breath of Childhood*. The book was a combination of Bronson's meditations on the growth of the spirit and his observations about childhood development. As Lizzie was an infant,

18. As an adult, Margaret is a doctor who works in the NICU, and I am still writing large and dramatic backstories for people who don't have them.

19. Bronson gave the manuscript to friend Ralph Waldo Emerson for his feedback; Emerson reluctantly informed him that the majority of the project was unpublishable, and Bronson eventually abandoned it.

she became the focus of the project, so much so the family called her "Psyche" for a time.

In its pages, Bronson Alcott sought to understand the mysterious alchemy occurring in his youngest daughter's mind. "I took [her] in my arms today that I might perchance tempt forth the indwelling vision and fix it for a moment on my own face," he wrote. "She fixed her eye on me with a deep intensity of vision. Yet a moment of endeavor, and the free will was disenthralled from the instinctive, and the vision was given her of living, individual being. Then came the smile—the sense—the upfilling joy—from the Spirit's life, from the fount whence cometh all love, all bliss, all peace, and repose that bloweth into the ample heart of man." He was also quite relieved at Lizzie's relative agreeableness, a trait that had apparently not manifested in his other children. She "cries but seldom; often smiles," he wrote, and "the prevailing temper of her spirit seems that of repose—deep, still, sustained peace. She is quiet, self-satisfied, self-subsistent. On the ocean of the Infinite doth her spirit calmly lie as a simple wavelet, unagitated by distant storms."

Bronson did not write this way about his other children. He recorded Anna calling for him after a terrifying and vivid dream; he noted his desire to take Louisa into the country so that he might access the "true history of [her spirit] . . . [her] range of thought, [her] vocabulary, [her] prevailing tendencies, whether good or evil." (May—the daughter after whom Amy would be modeled in *Little Women*—had yet to be born when *Psyche* was written.)

But as for Lizzie, her position was far more elemental:

This morning I saw Elizabeth," he wrote, "while her mother was preparing her for the day. The forms and motions of an infant—how beautiful! . . . How open were her arms! How confidingly did she stretch them forth toward that nature on whom she now relies for that sustaining influence which shall supply the waste and exhaustion of the animal functions of the flesh, into which she hath just entered! . . . Her position is, in itself, a prayer of aspiration; her breath life, an ascription. She hath faith; she hath love; she is bent heavenward. She turnest toward the source of the Spirit by the sense that worketh

deep within her, even as the sunflower towards
the radiant light on which it feeds!

Here, we can see Bronson's projections onto Lizzie,
the way he views her as having plantlike passivity, her
actions something akin to a Venus flytrap closing over
its prey. Pure instinct.

I am being unfair to Bronson. Of course he thought
of Elizabeth as a creature on whom he could project his
own mind; we adore imbuing newborns, like dogs, with
emotions and reactions that make sense to us. *He feels
guilty; she's having an existential crisis.* Plus, the other girls
were older, already exhibiting their own personalities.
Lizzie was an exquisite *tabula rasa*, an object with no
obvious subjectivity. "Psyche," Bronson wrote, "prefers
summertime."

In the story of Cupid and Psyche, Cupid was sent by
Venus to curse Psyche to love ugliness. But he accidentally scratched himself with his own arrow and fell in
love with her instead. Soon after, an oracle prophesied
to her parents that a terrible monster would wed their
daughter:

Let Psyche's corpse be clad in mourning weed
And set on rock of yonder hill aloft:
Her husband is no wight of human seed,
But serpent dire and fierce as may be thought,
Who flies with wings above in starry skies
And doth subdue each thing with fiery flight.
The gods themselves and powers that seem so wise
With mighty Jove be subject to his might;
The rivers black and deadly floods of pain
And darkness eke as thrall to him remain.

In terror, they send her to a cliffside. "As Psyche marches to the place of her exposure," writes Latin literature scholar Sophia Papaioannou, "[elaborate] rhetorical constructions are employed to emphasize the description of the funereal wedding and the coexistence of marriage and death . . . [once there, she] is exposed on the mountain and left there for a deadly marriage."[20] These ideas are "complementary aspects of a single experience, namely the transition to the unknown."

20. From "Charite's Rape, Psyche on the Rock and the Parallel Function of Marriage in Apuleius' 'Metamorphoses'" by Sophia Papaioannou.

"Beth's lingering death symbolizes the marriages of the remaining sisters," writes Athena Vrettos in her book *Somatic Fictions*, quoting the late feminist theorist Nina Auerbach. "Beth never matures because she does not seek access to a self-authorizing discourse. Her inability to construct a narrative identity[21] parallels her inability to leave the home, and invalidism becomes the logical extension of her domesticity . . . The fact that Beth's lingering death comes at the onset of adolescence allows her to retain her childhood identity amidst the changing structure of the March family."

In paintings of Psyche, she is classically beautiful: apple-breasted with skin like cream. Cupid is portrayed

21. Vrettos also points out that while "the strong, masculine Jo is the family 'scribbler,' making her way in the world through the art of storytelling, Beth is associated with the passive virtues of domesticity and silence. Beth is incapable of refiguring the world in fiction. . . . During a storytelling game at Laurie's picnic, Beth 'disappear[s] behind Jo,' leaving control of language to her more verbally dexterous sister. Whereas the other participants shape the interlocking stories to their own temperaments (Mr. Brooke fashions a tale of chivalrous knighthood; Meg a ghostly romance; Amy a fairy tale, and Jo a playful confusion of genres), Beth's life remains untransformed by linguistic play." Not only is she unable to locate herself as a character in a story, she is unable to tell a story, too.

either as a cherub—an infant—or an adolescent, and there is something very dark about their marriage: a beautiful woman claimed in holy matrimony by the concept of youth itself.

The scarlet fever chapter of *Little Women* is, I think, as close as Alcott gets to true, palpable horror. Beth talks in "a hoarse, broken voice," tries to sing through a swollen throat, runs her thin fingers over her blanket as if trying to play the piano, calls her sisters by the wrong names. She is in a "heavy stupor," her face "changed and vacant," her hands "weak and wasted," her "once-smiling lips quite dumb." Her illness is, for lack of a better word, creepy. It is "uncanny valley," dehumanizing. It is, like real illness and real death, terrifying, and gross.

But after this nightmarish period, the rest of Beth's death is positively Victorian: beautiful, holy, austere. In part two of *Little Women*, Jo observes that there is a "strange, transparent look about [Beth's face], as if the mortal was being slowly refined away, and the immortal shining through the frail flesh with an indescribably pathetic beauty." As it does in every film of the *Final Destination* franchise, the death that has been chasing her for so long draws near. Like the moment during her initial illness when she sat up and played the bedclothes on her lap like a piano, she hovers in the doorway between this world and another. There are many references to Beth as a "shadow," and this language appears also in describing Lizzie, in Louisa's journal, Abba's,[22] and Bronson's. It is easy to see why casting directors chose baby-faced, wide-eyed, peach-cheeked Claire Danes for Beth in the 1994 film adaptation—she was eerily adept at that ethereal plane.[23]

Late in the novel, Jo comes to believe that Beth has a big secret. After some deduction—including finding Beth weeping in the night—Jo concludes that her sister is in love with Laurie. "Jo mistakes Beth's pallor for the conventional signs of unrequited love," writes Vrettos, "[and her] first response is to try to write a new ending to Beth's story as she might for her own heroines, thereby

22. Upon Lizzie's death Abba wrote, "Elizabeth passed quietly into Shadow Land."

23. And, in Baz Luhrmann's *Romeo + Juliet* (1996), she expertly plays an utterly guileless young woman who is born with her fate firmly and tragically intact.

transforming the deathbed drama into a narrative of miraculous recovery." Only later, during a trip to the seaside, does she find out that—far from a crush—Beth has accepted that she is going to die, and soon. There, on the shore of her own metaphor, Beth says, "Every day I lose a little, and feel more sure that I shall never gain it back. It's like the tide, Jo, when it turns; it goes slowly, but it can't be stopped."

It is unfair to Louisa to be angry that she did not use *Little Women* to save her dear, dead sister. And yet it feels as if—as her father sealed Lizzie in the amber of his literary failure—Louisa did the same within her literary success. Infant or sweet or dying or dead, Lizzie never got the chance to belong to herself.

When I was in high school, a cyst that had grown on my ovary ruptured in the middle of algebra class. I raised my hand and asked to go to the nurse, but when I stood I screamed—a thin, involuntary sound. By the time I reached the nurse's office, my body was covered in a chilly film of moisture. My mother arrived and drove me to the hospital. She tried to carry me inside, for reasons I did not understand, but of course I was already too big for such a dramatic gesture and also, it wasn't necessary: they brought me a wheelchair.

I was fourteen that year. My mother's and my relationship had been precipitously crumbling for ages, and by the time she pushed me into that emergency room we were barely speaking to each other. She had correctly deduced that I was selfish and ungrateful, that I thought I was smarter than she was, that I had no respect for her. I was still years away from understanding my mother with any kind of psychological accuracy, but even then I knew that we existed on opposite sides of a great river. When I thought about my mother—the many judgments she made about me—something deep and ugly inside of me curdled. She wanted me to be permanently stunted—an infirm Peter Pan who called her regularly—and I did not want that for one second. I hated everything about her, and I told her as much, more than once.

In the ER, they did an ultrasound; my belly was full of fluid. I needed painkillers and rest, the doctor told my mother, and eventually my body would absorb it all, like a nightmarish ShamWow. My mother drove me home and grasped my elbow as I shuffled down the sidewalk and into the house.

I stayed on the couch until I could walk again, watch-

ing daytime TV until I fell asleep. My mother was curiously sweet and accommodating during those days;
her normal sharpness mellowed. I was reminded of
the long-ago best days of my small childhood with her
fussing over me, our conflicts forgotten. She liked being
needed, and I liked her that way. The scent of her per-
fume, indicating that she'd come into the room—it was
Cabotine de Grès, which takes its main notes from the
fickle Himalayan ginger lily—was soothing.

"You'll always need your mommy," she said once that
week, stroking my forehead while I convalesced on the
couch. The idea drifted through the fog of opioids and
landed in my silent contemplation. *No, I won't*, I thought.
Isn't that the point?

Maybe the question isn't *Are you a Beth?* Maybe the
question should be, *How do you keep other people from making you a Beth? How do you stay out of other people's stories?*

It's weirdly hard to dislike Beth; she's unflaggingly kind
and selfless. A bit Pollyanna-ish, sure, but ultimately a
force for good within the family. Alcott gives the tiniest
bit of lip service to Beth's human qualities—that is to say,
the normal difficulties that mark everyone—but they do
not emerge on the page. Beth does not rage against the

unfairness of her situation; but even worse than that, she *wants nothing.* It is impossible to imagine her adulthood. Not even just the reader; Beth can't imagine it, either. "I only mean to say that I have a feeling that it never was intended I should live long," she tells Jo, shortly before the end of her life. "I'm not like the rest of you. I never made any plans about what I'd do when I grew up. I never thought of being married, as you all did. I couldn't seem to imagine myself anything but stupid little Beth, trotting about at home, of no use anywhere but there."

Lizzie's doctor's final diagnosis for her was "atrophy or consumption of the nervous system, with great development of hysteria." It is hard, when thinking about Lizzie, not to also think of Alice James—younger sister of psychiatrist William James and author Henry James. Lizzie's father, Bronson, and Alice's, Henry James Sr., were contemporaries and acquaintances who moved in the same New England circles. Like Lizzie, Alice was an invalid, diagnosed with a litany of ailments common to women at the time, including neurasthenia[24] and hyste-

---

24. Muttonchopped nineteenth-century neurologist George Beard, who coined the term "neurasthenia," believed that the condition could in part be blamed on "an increase of mental activity among women," a symptom of the modern age.

ria. Like Lizzie, she would die young, and recede into her famous family's long shadow.

Unlike Lizzie, Alice kept extensive letters and diaries that showcase her brilliance and wit, even though it would take half a century for people to begin to acknowledge it. Unfortunately, there are not many surviving letters or diaries[25] belonging to Lizzie Alcott, though whether that's because they were lost, or because she did not write or keep them with any regularity, is unclear. But the writing of Lizzie's that survives is wry and dark and creates a sketch of a fierce and funny woman managing her situation as best she can. In one letter, sent to her family from Boston where she was convalescing at the home of a family friend, she tells of her journey there:

> A woman put her head in very saucily to inquire
> if I was an invalid and [if] I had been sick long.
> She stared her fill and not discomposing myself
> at all I stared at her. She soon retired, [and] I

25. In one journal—kept in 1846, when she was ten—she mostly wrote of poetry memorized and words learned, of her sewing and walks and the weather. On September 29 of that year, a Tuesday, Lizzie wrote, "After dinner, I washed the dishes and [Abba] and I played in [her] chamber. I was a sick lady and Abba was a doctor."

reposed quite nicely at my ease and though my head ached did not feel as much as I thought. Ate my chicken with a relish and troubled myself about nobody.

Later, she writes of a "Miss Hinkley"—presumably a nurse—who "was horridly shocked at my devouring meat . . . and stared her big eyes at me. [She] will probably come to deliver another lecture soon. I don't care for the old cactus a bit." At the letter's closing, Lizzie implored them all to "write often to [their] little skeleton."

Reading these letters, and imagining Lizzie's dead-eyed stare at nosy women on public transit and over-bearing, fussing nurses—imagining her eating with relish and troubling herself about no one at all—I feel a kind of mourning setting in. More than thinking about beautiful, kind, faultless Beth, who chatted endlessly about goodness and piety and nothing at all, I imagine instead this wasted young woman—barely ninety pounds, her hair falling out, so goth she married death itself—calling herself a "little skeleton," and chuckling at her own dark joke.

Of course I didn't always need my mommy. I did not want her narrative for my life. I actively rejected it.

In my day-to-day—my relationships, my friendships, my education, my job—I progressed along a normal path. I made my own choices, some good (grad school, thoughtfully selected tattoos), some bad (a string of unfortunate significant others, an ill-advised pixie cut). I started a career and got engaged and made my student loan payments every month and got married. But for some reason—a reason I never fully understood—my mother seemed to think I was permanently fourteen years old. "But you hate needles," my mother said to me when I was in my mid-twenties, and I encouraged her to get a flu shot by telling her I'd gotten my own.

"I don't love them," I said, "but I get shots all of the time. I haven't been scared of needles in ages."

"But you won't let anyone near you with a syringe," she said.

"Yeah," my sister echoed. "Remember how they tried to take your blood when you were a kid and six fat nurses had to hold you down?" Ah yes, the six fat nurses: identical and round and probably wearing jaunty mid-century nurses' caps. Archetypal, misremembered unto fictional.

"That's how I used to be," I said. "I'm not like that anymore."

"I'm your mother," my mother said. "I know you better than you know yourself."

This idea—that my mother knew that a young version of myself was more *me* than me, and that only she had access to that knowledge—bothered me so much I couldn't stop thinking about it. What a thing to say. What a thing for a mother to say to her adult child who she rarely sees.

When I brought it up to my therapist, he drew upon the metaphor of a seesaw. It is possible, he explained, to make a seesaw sit level. As long as the participants on either side are the same weight, and sit in the same way, they will both be facing each other. But the minute that changes—the minute someone leans back or kicks off from the ground—the equality is altered. "When children become adults," he said, "there's an unspoken pact. Even though you were, once, a kid, you aren't anymore, and your relationship has to change, or else it won't. The minute one person acts like the kid, or one person acts like the kid's parent, the balance shifts and you revert to the dynamic of your old relationship." In other words, if you are the sort of person who needs an adult to remain a child, it is possible, through narrative, to keep him or her that way.

I don't know how I would have turned out if I'd let my mother keep shaping my narrative. After all, Lizzie's family had a narrative about her, and it killed her. Not just once, but over and over again. A woman who lived and had thoughts and made art and was snarky and strange and funny and kind and suffered tremendously and died angry at the world becomes sweet, soft Beth. A dear, and nothing else.

When she was a baby and sat playing on the floor of the family home, Lizzie's older sisters built a tower of books around her. She was so agreeable about it, they kept going until she was entirely concealed. Then—losing interest in the game—they wandered away and forgot about her. When the Alcott family discovered that baby Lizzie was missing, they searched and searched. Eventually they found her "curled up and fast asleep in her dungeon cell," Louisa wrote in her journal. "[She] emerged so rosy and smiling after her nap that we were forgiven for our carelessness."

There are so many ways to read this story. Lizzie as inherently passive. Lizzie as a good-natured child. Lizzie as a character in a novel engaging in some good, old-fashioned foreshadowing. That last one is the one I cannot shake: Lizzie sitting obediently as her family built a sepulcher of words around her.

JANE SMILEY ON AMY

I AM YOUR "PRUDENT AMY"

WHEN I WAS growing up (I think I first read *Little Women* when I was ten) I identified with Jo—she was tall, she was literary, and she represented Alcott herself. Her journey is the most prominent of the four. But now, when I look at the girls, the one I enjoy the most is Amy.

When we meet the March sisters on page one, it is Christmas and there are no presents because of the Civil War—lack of funds, frightening absence of Father. Each girl responds to the news characteristically—Jo (aged 15) grumbles, Meg (16) sighs, Amy (12) offers "an injured sniff," and Beth (13 to 14) speaks last, "contentedly." The four girls then recollect that each of them has saved a bit of money, about a dollar (maybe $19.00 now). Meg says that she would like to buy herself some "pretty things." Jo wants a copy of a book of two fantastical stories translated from German, one about a water sprite, the other about a knight. Beth would like some music (she is the pianist), and Amy says, "decidedly," that she wants drawing pencils. None of the four seems more selfish than the others at this point, but the next passage is revealing. Each sister now issues a complaint—Meg about the children she takes care of, Jo about her "fussy" aunt, whom she also tends to, Beth about her household tasks (though she doesn't like to complain). Amy, who is the only one who goes to school, makes the most modern complaint—at twelve, she is surrounded by other twelve-year-olds. She says, "I don't believe any of you suffer as I do, for you don't have to go to school with impertinent girls, who plague you if you don't know your lessons, and laugh at your dresses, and label your father if he isn't rich, and insult you when your nose isn't nice" (by "label" Amy means "libel"). Because she negotiates the social world of what would now be junior high school, Amy is (and must be) always aware not only of her own feelings but of her social status and how she appears.

In fact, Jo and Amy constitute two types of feminists we will see in the future who will agree on some matters and disagree on others—Jo is the one who values her independence and wishes to retain it even if it leads to disagreement or unhappiness; Amy is the one who thinks that the best option for doing what she wants is to learn to navigate and make use of the world she is stuck with. We might think of Jo as the "agitator," Amy as the "political operative."

It is no surprise that of the four, Jo and Amy are the two who are most often at odds with one another. One reason is that, as every novelist knows, and as Alcott herself knew, all four of the sisters cannot be good—readers with their own daughters and sisters wouldn't buy it and if there was no conflict, no character development, the plot would have nothing to build upon. Meg has a few faults, but she must end up as the wife and mother. Beth has no faults—she is the sacrificial victim (and realistically so, since many nineteenth-century children died before they reached adulthood). Jo is the central character who needs a foil, and Amy is it. If she is going to be a worthy foil, she needs to be as complex as Jo—as ready to learn, though in different ways, and as ready to do battle so that their conflict will force them to learn from their experiences. She can't be a flat character, and she isn't—though as the youngest, most petted sister she is often seen by her sisters (and by readers) as vain, calculating, and spoiled—she actually has the self-awareness and reflectiveness that will help her navigate the adult world.

Alcott was inspired by John Bunyan's sixteenth-century allegory *The Pilgrim's Progress*—her epigraph makes this explicit in directing the reader's attention to the less-often-read book two of *The Pilgrim's Progress*, the story of Christiana, her young neighbor Mercy, and Christiana's children as they journey to the Celestial City—but instead of medieval women on pilgrimage, her subjects were modern girls living in the modern world. Their job is to negotiate real events—war, poverty, family life, career aspirations, and, of course, growing into womanhood. But what is their goal? Marmee would say that it is to be kind, self-sacrificing, womanly, generous, to marry, have children, and serve others, and indeed they do, when they get to the Hummels' shack: Hannah builds the fire, Marmee tends to the mother and baby, and Meg, Jo, Beth, and Amy (who has offered to "'. . . take the cream and the muffins,' . . . heroically giving up the articles she most liked") lay out the provisions and feed the hungry children. Their Christmas is merry and their lesson is a religious one, as Meg understands: the lesson of loving thy neighbor.

Alcott's theory of child development is specifically

Christian, as were most American theories of child development until the early twentieth century. Marmee's goal is to get Meg, Jo, Beth, and Amy to adhere to a set of general principles. She chooses to do it through kind persuasion rather than force, and the two parts of *Little Women* constitute a demonstration of how that system works. Marmee's job is not the one most modern American mothers take on: to investigate the individuality of her children, to contemplate their differences and decide if their qualities are a product of nature or nurture. It never occurs to Marmee to wonder if the chaos of having four daughters in four years, and in moderate circumstances, has caused those daughters to develop in idiosyncratic ways. As a mother, I would have told her that Amy was certainly shaped by, and has in some ways benefited from, the inevitable neglect she would have experienced as a baby and a toddler when her sisters were five, four, and two—she would have had plenty of time on her own to explore her world and think her own thoughts. Those of us with several children know that she would also have had to avoid being bullied, to protect her toys and her other possessions from the older girls, and to assert herself from time to time.

Alcott herself was from an interesting family that

had strong convictions—her uncle, Samuel J. May, was a prominent Unitarian minister and abolitionist leader, and her mother, Abigail May, together with Alcott's father, Bronson, dedicated their lives to social reform, the abolition of slavery, and the promotion of temperance, women's rights, and aid to the poor. Bronson was famous (or infamous) for classroom innovations that would now seem progressive—Socratic (rather than prescriptive) discussions of hot-button issues, like the meaning of biblical stories, or having students explore their own experiences through writing about them. His experimental schools and the books he wrote describing his unconventional teaching methods garnered significant criticism and no money. Around the time that May Alcott (the model for Amy) was born, the family was living in Concord, Massachusetts, and being supported by Ralph Waldo Emerson. When Louisa was ten, Bronson bought some property and attempted to establish an ideal agrarian community—no meat, no animal labor, no leather or fabrics that were grown by means of slave labor (cotton, silk, wool). The new experiment lasted seven months. This idealism and family background had a strong influence on Louisa. She herself later said that she had a powerful religious experience (though she never officially joined a church):

> "Running in the Concord woods early one fall morning, she stopped to see the sunshine over the meadows. 'A very strange and solemn feeling came over me as I stood there,' she wrote in her journal, 'with no sound but the rustle of the pines, no one near me, and the sun so glorious, as for me alone. It seemed as if I felt God as I never did before, and I prayed in my heart that I might keep that happy sense of nearness all my life.'"*

When a publisher suggested to her in 1867 that she write a book for girls, she realized that as an unmarried woman with no children, she didn't particularly like girls, so she turned to her own experiences for material. When she sat down to write *Little Women*, she recalled the precepts that her mother had employed to raise her and her sisters while contending with the chaos produced by her

---

*"Louisa May Alcott," Dictionary of Unitarian and Universalist Biography, uub.org.

principled and eccentric father, and she also pulled from the actual lives of herself and her three sisters. By the time Louisa was writing *Little Women*, May was in her mid-twenties, and had spent much of her life learning to teach children or teaching them. She was an active artist, studied when she was in her late teens at the School of the Museum of Fine Arts, in Boston, and she also supplied the illustrations for *Little Women* as well as publishing her own art book, called *Concord Sketches*. Like Louisa, she was single, and she remained single until she was in her late thirties.

Perhaps the first in-depth exploration of Amy's experiences, and also the first hurdle Amy must confront in her path to self-knowledge, comes in chapter seven. In order to claim some status at her school, Amy thinks she must share with the other girls a treat that is the latest craze, pickled limes (which are limes preserved in salt). Meg gives her a quarter, worth maybe five dollars today; Amy buys some, and carries them to school in a brown paper bag. Then comes a classic episode of bullying that every modern girl can recognize—she gets some praise from her teacher for maps she has drawn, and the girl who envies the praise tattles to the teacher about the pickled limes. Amy is called to the front of the room, forced to throw the limes out the window, then subjected to having her hand smacked with a ruler. The pain is not as great as the humiliation, and, perhaps thinking of Bronson Alcott's educational principles, Alcott writes, "during the twelve years of her life she had been governed by love alone, and a blow of that sort had never touched her." Since physical punishment, sometimes brutal, was routine in the nineteenth century (and stories from my own relatives born in the 1880s and '90s attest to this), this line is perhaps the most radical in the book so far—I don't think most of us in the twenty-first century understand how fundamental whipping and humiliation were to nineteenth-century educational theories and practices. Marmee "comforts" Amy by criticizing her: "You are getting to be altogether too conceited and important, my dear, and it is quite time you set about correcting it. You have a good many little gifts and virtues, but there is no need of parading them, for conceit spoils the finest genius." It is true that Amy took the pickled limes to school in order to elevate her status. But it was showing off by giving gifts, not preening or bragging. I, perhaps, am more forgiving than Marmee is. Amy then voices the lesson she has learned from the events in her chapter: "I see, it's nice to have accomplishments, and be elegant, but not to show off, or get perked up."

What would I, a twentieth- and twenty-first-century mother, have done and said in similar circumstances? In the first place, Marmee never addresses the real crime, which was the envious reporting of the limes by the other student. She seems to believe that bullying and backstabbing are so much the norm that the only thing a bullied child can do is turn the other cheek. Jo does take a letter to the teacher and Amy does leave the school, but Marmee never talks to Amy about the injustice, except to suggest that maybe she deserved it. When my own children were bullied in school, I went to the teachers and the principal, and they attempted to rein in the bullies, not the bullied. In addition, perhaps because my eighth grade history teacher wrote on my report card, "She only does what she wants to do," thinking that was a bad thing, I would also have told Marmee that focus, desire, determination, and resistance, qualities that Amy has, are what lead to accomplishment and self-realization.

We are now just under a third of the way into the novel, but even though Jo is the principal character, we have seen enough of Amy to understand that she has potential that the others, even Marmee, don't yet perceive.

The next person to hurt Amy's feelings is Jo, who, Amy discovers, is planning to go with Meg and Laurie to a play at a nearby theater. Amy knows of the show and wants to accompany the others, but the older girls don't simply tell her that there aren't enough tickets or that the seats have already been reserved, they disdain her— Jo says, "Little girls shouldn't ask questions," and Meg, though speaking more kindly, says, "be a good child." Amy is enraged and calls out, "You'll be sorry for this, Jo March, see if you ain't." Everything seems fine when they get home; Jo checks her things because Amy has a history of vengeful acts and a previous argument had ended in Amy pulling out the top drawer of Jo's dresser and upending it. Alcott writes that both girls have "quick tempers." What Amy has done this time is much more serious, though—she has burned the manuscript Jo has been working on. After confessing, she shows no immediate remorse and Jo grabs her and shakes her "till her teeth chattered in her head." Amy then attempts to apologize but her apology is rejected. Marmee stays out of it, knowing that Jo has to back away from her anger on her own (and if I had discovered that one of my children shook the other one until her teeth chattered, I would have NOT stayed out of it). The next day, Jo and Laurie leave Amy behind once again, when they go skating on the nearby river. Amy wants to go along and Meg advises her to do so, thinking that Laurie and the exercise will put Jo in a better mood. When Amy follows them to the river, Jo ignores her. Because Amy is not very near the older kids and is concentrating on putting on her skates and catching up with Jo, she doesn't hear Laurie warn about the fragile ice away from the banks. The worst thing that Jo does is ignore her own conscience, thinking, "No matter whether she heard or not, let her take care of herself." Jo's punishment is instantaneous: the ice breaks, Amy falls through into "the black water." It is Laurie who saves Amy, with Jo's help. After they get Amy home and she is safe in bed, Alcott devotes the rest of the chapter to Jo's conversation with Marmee about what Jo needs to learn about controlling her temper. What seems to be overlooked is not only Amy's pain and fear, but also that Amy never again acts out of rage or thoughtlessness—as usual, she learns her lesson on her own, and the lesson is that if anyone is going to take care of her, it must be herself. If these were my daughters, I would have postponed my conversation with Jo, spent time with Amy, comforting her and watching her for evidence of PTSD, brought them together for a conversation about both the burned manuscript and what Jo has done, and then explained very clearly to both of them that they must learn to control their tempers. I would have given them some advice: take a few deep breaths before you speak, walk away if you can't control yourself, have a conversation, not a fight, come to me with a complaint so that I can help you negotiate.

A few pages later, Marmee details her hopes and dreams for her daughters to Meg and Jo—she wants them "to be beautiful, accomplished, and good; to be admired, loved, and respected." In other words, the first thing she wants—or the first thing she thinks of—is that she wants them to be seen by others in a positive way, to achieve social standing in a physical way, an intellectual way, and a moral way, in that order. Meg and Jo then draw her out, and the conversation turns to marriage—should it be for money, or not for money? All three of them recognize that a nineteenth-century woman's economic comfort is not often in her own hands, that most women have to marry to support themselves, and Marmee is very specific when she says, "I'd rather see you poor men's wives, if you were happy, beloved, contented, than queens on thrones, without self-respect and peace." It is Jo who voices Alcott's own choice: "Then we'll be old maids." Someone has to, because Alcott herself was an "old maid." Meg is destined by her author to be the happy, beloved, and contented poor man's wife, and so Jo and Amy have two choices between them. They must decide which one of them is to be the old maid, and which the rich man's wife.

I do not remember receiving any advice from my mother, or giving any advice to my daughters, about overarching goals—what I wanted was for them to have goals of their own, and the way they were to discover them was through education. My mother read my report cards, made sure I did my homework, went to teacher-parent conferences, encouraged reading and going to the library; I did the same with my daughters. The path to womanhood was through the corridors at school and on the playground, where we learned to socialize with the other students and navigate the larger world. My job as a girl was to look around and decide what I wanted to do, what I was able to do, and how these two things might be combined. I thought that my job as a mother was not to think of beauty first, or even admiration, it was to think of effort, of proper behavior, of thought, of ambition. I did not think about my children growing up to be "good"—I knew that if they were good now, they would be good as adults. As her mother, I would not have taken Amy out of her school, or if I had, I would have found her another. Once Amy is removed from the school, her growing understanding of the social world must become more random, less productive. But she keeps at it because she is smart enough to understand that she has to in order to grow up and also to get what she wants.

In this way, too, Amy is more modern than her sisters. She goes about shaping her life in a conscious manner that seems calculated to the other girls. For example, as *Little Women* unfolds, a lot of attention is given to Jo's literary efforts, because whatever they are, and Jo herself admits they are trashy, they help support the family.

Amy is just as dedicated to her own artistic efforts—in chapter four, Alcott writes that her sisters call her "Little Raphael" and that she has "a decided talent for drawing, and was never so happy as when copying flowers, designing fairies, or illustrating stories with queer specimens of art." Let's say that if I were her mother, I would not say "queer," I would say "original," but as time passes, her efforts come to be seen by the other members of her family as a demonstration of vanity, partly because she would rather make "mud pies" than do housework. Her taste improves—she moves on from mud pies to drawing, "poker art," and painting. But the family needs money, and Jo's popular magazine stories do make some, while Amy's efforts make none. The "mud pies" reveal something about Amy, even though the words are a bit derogative—she knows that in order to learn, she has to make do with materials that the family can afford. The others might be amused at her efforts, but she knows what any artist would tell her—that practice of any kind is productive. Once again a modern woman in the making, she wants to find a way to express herself. We can compare her efforts to Jo's literary ones—Jo writes her pulp fiction tales to make money, without thinking about whether she is expressing her own inner life. Since Amy is learning, and not making money, she focuses on developing her vision and her skills.

When the girls' father is injured in the Civil War, and Marmee and Mr. Brooke must go to him, leaving the girls in the care of the family maid and cook, Hannah, the girls discuss how they will handle their unease. Jo says, "'Hope and keep busy;' that's the motto for us." Meg is vexed about having to go to her child-care job; she would rather help around the house. Amy "with an important air" declares that she, Beth, and Hannah can take care of the house, and then, taking a bit of sugar, she adds what I consider to be one of her most revealing remarks, "I think anxiety is very interesting." The other girls can't help laughing in response. But what Amy is showing is a penchant for introspection, for weighing all aspects of her temperament—her feelings, her desires, her needs, her obligations—and sorting them out so that she can learn from them. As a youngest child who must observe her three older sisters, as well as Marmee, Hannah, and her other relatives, she has a large amount of data to sort through—youngest children may be dismissed, but they cannot dismiss. They are forced to contemplate the psychology of the others—what works, what doesn't work, what they can or cannot get away with, and how they might push that envelope subtly and effectively. Amy already knows that bribery—that is, pickled limes—and revenge—the burned manuscript—don't work. As she grows up, she recognizes that what does work is a combination of charm, determination, and self-knowledge. These qualities are demonstrated in her letter to Marmee in chapter sixteen. Alcott makes fun of her a bit by including her misspellings and vanities (one of which is signing a letter to her own mother with her formal name, "Amy Curtis March"), but as silly as the letter is intended to be (she writes, "Meg says my punchtuation and spelling are disgraceful and I am mortyfied but dear me I have so many things to do I can't stop"), it is clear even in its single paragraph that Amy is interested in behaving properly, feeling calm and comforted, having an indulgence or two, not being teased (by Laurie), dressing correctly, taming her own feelings of dissatisfaction, organizing her activities, and expressing love for her parents. Amy is the only sister who comes to understand that anxiety can be enlightening if she is willing to examine its sources.

When Beth comes down with scarlet fever, Amy happens not to be nearby. Meg and Jo agree to care for Beth, and Amy, because she hasn't had scarlet fever, is sent away, over her objections, to Aunt March, their father's wealthy aunt. At first Amy is lonely and resentful—she realizes "how much she was beloved and petted at home." Jo had been tending to Aunt March as a way of earning some money, but did not get along with her and was resentful of Aunt March's rules and crotchets. Amy begins with the same attitude, but in fact, Aunt March likes Amy because she is "more docile and amiable" than Jo. I would say that Amy's behavior is not so much docile and amiable—those words imply that Amy dissembles in order to get along with her great-aunt—as it is thoughtful and reserved, owing to her desire to learn from her new surroundings. She is now being exposed to a different, and more elegant, culture than the one she knows at home, in part because Aunt March has money, but also through Esther, Aunt March's French maid. Esther not only tells Amy about France, Catholicism, and her own upbringing, she also shows her Aunt March's treasures: her diamonds, her pearls, and her turquoise ring, which is the one Amy likes the most. Esther, in the true Balzac tradition, reveals to Amy that she has witnessed Aunt March's will, and knows that the jewels are going to the March sisters after she dies. When, as a result of this, Amy becomes the "docile and amiable" attendant Aunt March desires, her new behavior is morally complex— Jo's resistance to her aunt, by comparison, is presented as an honorable assertion that her aunt can't buy her off. But if Amy were my daughter, forced to live with a disagreeable relative because of a family crisis, I would advise her to find ways to get along, to try to understand the complexities of her aunt's psychology, to please her as a way of making her not only more agreeable, but happier. Family conflict is not merely a financial issue. If there really was an Aunt March in the Alcott family, perhaps it was she who was offended by Bronson Alcott's peculiarities, and what she longed for was a relation she could like and care for. Amy is a realist— she thinks the ring is beautiful and would like to have it—her artistic endeavors show that she is attracted and moved by beauty. But she also knows that what she is learning by living with Aunt March and Esther is worthwhile because her sense of the world is being expanded and enriched.

Amy again internalizes her lesson, this time by writing her own will, which the others go along with as if it is a pleasant joke. But the will is a sign of Amy's constantly growing understanding of how the world works—she knows, because of her father's illness, the Hummel baby's death, and Beth's illness, that death is a constant threat that can strike suddenly. She knows that she has possessions that she values and that she wishes for her relatives to value, and she knows that being thoughtful and organized is the best option. When she decides how she is going to distribute her legacy, she also takes a stab at understanding the desires of her friends and relatives and leaves them, along with other things, what she thinks they would most desire. When she is discussing the will with Laurie, who is evidently humoring her, she adds what she calls "a postscript," though Laurie corrects her, telling her it is a "codicil." After she dies, she would like to have her hair cut and locks given to everyone—she not only knows that her hair, thick, curly, and golden, is her glory, she also knows that she would like to be remembered as a person, not merely as a producer of art. Her will shows that Amy has the wisdom and self-knowledge to plan for the possibility of death. Then, when Laurie tells her that Beth's illness remains serious, she secretly goes into the chapel she and Esther have built, and prays, with tears, for Beth's recovery, demonstrating that she has plenty of feelings that she is wary of revealing, unlike Jo, who habitually acts on impulse.

The day Marmee comes home, Beth recovers from her bout of scarlet fever, and Laurie is sent to Aunt March's house to tell Amy the good news. Amy's first thought is that her private prayers have paid off. Marmee appears and Amy takes her to her private "chapel" and explains how she has been making use of it. For once Marmee is approving, but her approval only lasts until she sees the turquoise ring that Aunt March has given her. She says, "I think you're rather young for such ornaments, Amy." By this time, perhaps because of those hours of introspection the chapel represents, Amy has enough self-knowledge to respond that the ring is not a display, but a reminder to not be selfish. Marmee is amused, though she hides her amusement. But what Amy says to her mother demonstrates that the arc of her particular plot has been accomplished. It is not exactly that she has learned not to be vain or selfish, but that she has figured out a way to coordinate all of her ambitions. The ring symbolizes not only what she knows, but also what she wants and how she can go about getting it. She understands that investigating her feelings and molding her fears and desires in private (the chapel) can lead to understanding and getting along with others, including others who are wealthy and powerful, namely Aunt March and Laurie.

How she contrasts with Jo in this is evident in the next requirement of the plot, which is getting Meg married off to Laurie's tutor, John Brooke. Amy plays no part in the brouhaha between Aunt March and Meg that causes Meg to realize that she does love John and does wish to marry him (Aunt March is offended that Meg refuses to marry for money), but Amy's final observation demonstrates her way of looking at things: "'You can't say "nothing pleasant ever happens now," can you, Meg?' said Amy, trying to decide how she would group the lovers in the sketch she was planning to make." Her role is to observe, to weigh one event against the other, to figure out how to represent the events and the feelings in her chosen art form in a way that will make sense of them both for herself and others. By the end of part one, Meg has learned to love, Jo has learned to accept that her impulsive desires can't always be fulfilled, Beth has learned to survive. Amy is now thirteen, and if she were my daughter, I would say that her mind works in a sophisticated way—she has learned the most subtle and perhaps the most important lesson, to pay attention.

Part two begins three years later, when Meg is old enough to get married. Jo is now earning some money with her writing; Laurie has gone to college and has an active social life among the local privileged young men. Amy is sixteen, and has become "quite a belle" (which might be simultaneously a recognition of her beauty and a gentle mockery of her desires to fit into the social world). Alcott is straightforward about how Amy's response to Laurie's friends differs from Jo's—Jo feels so much like one of them that it seems natural to her to behave as they do. They like her, but "never fell in love with her." A few of them give Amy the sort of attention that young men of social standing in the nineteenth century accorded to attractive but well-protected young women, "paying the tribute of a sentimental sigh or two at Amy's shrine" (another small joke). Amy knows her role is to be appealing but remote, to lure them with her looks and behavior but never allow them to think she can be claimed. A signal of her power is that she "dared to order them about," which surprises Beth. The only things that give her this power, since the March family have very little money or social standing, are her self-possession, her looks, and her choice to be assertive.

In some ways, the central character of part two is Laurie. Now that he is out of school and launched into the social world of wealth, he is in danger of wasting his time, wasting his money, or becoming dissolute. Throughout the two parts, he demonstrates many good qualities—he is generous, affectionate, kind, exuberant, and willing to learn (though sometimes he has to be prodded to do so). His main problem is that he has no sense of purpose, unlike every one of the March girls. Alcott implies that this is the effect of too much money, but also the effect of losing his own parents, and therefore having no strong models of respectable choices. School does not give him a goal or a mission—and there are no passages in the novel about how Laurie experiences his schooling other than as a way to connect with other young men of his social class; college is more of a club than a library. His grandfather is not really in a position to save him, so his redemption falls to the Marches. Alcott's somewhat implausible narrative task is to keep him in the family, because he is a main character in the novel and is charming—to marry him off to some random girl would mean that this young woman would have to be incorporated into a group of young women we know very well—would she be a source of conflict or estrangement? Would she have her own point of view, her own issues that would cause plot twists or digressions? If she did not fit in in a believable way, then Laurie would have to be abandoned as a principal character. But who must he marry to stay in the family?

It cannot be Meg, because her marriage must demonstrate Marmee's thoughts about how ideal marriages work.

It cannot be Beth, because she is too sickly to take on marital responsibilities and because she must die.

Readers of part one—and there were lots of them since it was a huge success—wanted Laurie to marry Jo, but Alcott herself was not married, and did not want the character she based upon herself to betray her own sense of independence.

So the only one left was Amy, and Alcott's narrative task was to make this marriage not only believable but interesting.

The fact that Amy has developed into "the flower of the family" does not spare her from having the same sort of humiliating experience in the third chapter of part two that she had in part one with the pickled limes. She has been diligently working on her art, and has been taking a drawing class with some other girls. At the end of the semester (as we would call it), she decides to invite the other girls to a "fête," so elaborately planned that Jo, hard at work on her novel, is annoyed. She exclaims, "Why in the world should you spend your money, worry your family, and turn the house upside down for a parcel of girls who don't care a sixpence for you?" And in fact the fête does go wrong—only one of the girls shows up, but Amy and her family entertain her and the other girl has a good time in the end. Jo's response to Amy's failed plans is laughter, Marmee's is regret at Amy's disappointment, but this time, Amy is not disappointed—she says, "I *am* satisfied; I've done what I undertook, and it's not my fault that it failed." And she seems to have learned the same thing with regard to her strenuous artistic endeavors, described earlier in the chapter: she has made use of the materials at hand, including hand-me-down paints and palettes and local scenery; she has taught herself to keep trying—slow and steady, the tortoise rather than the hare. Could Amy, too, make money from her work and help support the family? Jo—now a successful writer—provides Amy with the model. Might Amy too have a publishing career? It is possible that she could illustrate books or draw cartoons for newspapers. But once again, Amy's function as a character is to provide contrast with Jo, if only because the reader would turn away if both characters made the same choices, had the same ambitions. As a "political operative" rather than an "agitator," Amy aims with her art to express her individuality, but also make use of the system, not wreck it. Artists who make use of the system, as I have done as a realistic novelist and as May did as a realistic painter, want to depict and critique what they observe, to pass it through their own consciousness and present it to the reader or the viewer. They find the world around themselves ever more interesting as they focus upon it. Jo, as a writer of fantasy stories, is more interested in making use of emotions like fear and dread to excite her readers.

In the sixth chapter of part two, Amy begins organizing Jo, something I have seen younger siblings do,
and usually in the reasonable manner that a smaller and
weaker person must adopt. Meg has attempted to do it by
example, Marmee with good advice, Beth by sweetness,
and Aunt March with impatience and sharp reproaches,
but Jo continues to be outspoken, impulsive, and not
especially feminine. Amy knows that social interaction is
worthwhile and productive; she pushes Jo to fulfill a bargain she has made to accompany Amy on "half a dozen
calls" (social visits to neighbors) in return for a sketch
Amy made of Beth. Amy understands, as she did about
the fête, that being well connected is valuable, whether
or not all of the connections are pleasant (perhaps this is
the lesson she learned from having to put up with Aunt
March as well as from going to school). She also knows
that Jo needs practice repaying her end of the bargain.
Amy's method of reforming Jo is debate—Jo uses several
arguments in an attempt to weasel out of the calls—and
then Amy's response sounds like one a mother or an
older sister might make, telling Jo how to dress, how
to behave, why they are making this effort, but doing
so with much patience and some flattery, keeping at it
until Jo has been guided to the first call. Jo, of course,

uses the first call to make fun of Amy's assertions: she adopts a stylish demeanor but doesn't say anything, leading the woman they have called upon, Mrs. Chester, to declare that she is "haughty" and "uninteresting"—the sisters overhear her remark as they leave the house (Jo has caused annoyance, as agitators do). But Amy keeps at it in spite of her own feelings of disappointment. The first benefit of their day of visits is that they have a long conversation as they walk from house to house, making progress in their understanding of one another, and the second, as it turns out, is that no matter how hard she tries, Amy cannot make Jo understand how to be agreeable, and so Amy unexpectedly profits by her contrast with her sister. Their last visit is to Aunt March and Aunt Carroll, who are discussing something that they set aside when the girls appear. The hint is when the two women ask Jo and Amy about their language skills. Jo says that she is "very stupid about studying anything" and that she "can't bear French, it's such a slippery, silly sort of language." Amy says that she has learned a lot of French from Esther, Aunt March's French maid, and that she is grateful for it. The die is cast.

As the only one of the girls whose job is to navigate

the social world, Amy faces challenges that get larger
and more complex. Having impressed Mrs. Chester
during their social visit, she is invited to be part of a
"fair" to support the freedmen after the end of the Civil
War, an event where various tables are set up and staffed
by well-dressed socially prominent young women about
Amy's age. Amy begins at one of the prominent tables,
but is suddenly and unaccountably moved to the flower
table, on the periphery. The first day doesn't go well
and Amy is disheartened, but when Marmee, Jo, and
Laurie find out what has happened, Laurie comes to the
rescue by having his gardener supply her the second
day with "a wilderness of flowers." The March family
and Laurie and his friends surround her table, buy the
flowers, make her spot the liveliest at the fair and the
most profitable. Jo not only amuses people visiting the
table, she also walks around, scouting for information,
and discovers that May Chester, Mrs. Chester's daughter, about Amy's age, has betrayed her because she was
jealous that Amy had been given the prominent table.
May apologizes, apparently sincerely, and then Laurie's
friends go to her table and buy her goods, too. The result
is not departure, as when Amy leaves the school after

the limes incident, or quiet acceptance, as when Amy acknowledges the failure of her fête by being satisfied that she at least did her job, but general reconciliation, pleasure, and success. Amy has learned to navigate the specifically female social world by making the best of her assigned place, but also enlisting allies and putting on a good face. She ends up not only being accepted, but having an enjoyable day. The other girls all praise her; Marmee says nothing, and if I had been in the room, I wouldn't have said anything either—Amy's lesson has been learned by all of them.

Then Aunt Carroll sends a letter, inviting Amy along on a trip to Europe. Jo and Amy now have to work out whatever feelings of conflict or jealousy Jo feels about Amy's fulfillment of a wish that Jo has also had for a long time. Jo asserts that Amy will have "all the fun" when she first finds out about the invitation. Amy tells Jo what she hopes to do—to practice her art and find out, once and for all, whether she has any "genius"—she is looking for inspiration and to understand herself and she plans to work hard at it. Like a modern young woman embarking on an independent life, she is also thinking about her other options, as she always does, as she has learned to do—if she has no genius, she is well aware that she can become an art teacher, or she can marry a wealthy man and fund artists who do have genius. Alcott uses their conversation to illustrate Amy's and Jo's different but reasonable approaches to making their lives. Their conversation goes directly to one of the major differences between them: money. Jo is the one who writes popular fiction for money, Amy is the one who scrapes together what materials she can find to pursue her artistic ambitions and makes no money, as yet. Jo's moneymaking is seen as a necessity so that the Marches can get by. But because Amy dresses well, behaves properly, and gets along with Aunt March, and because, unlike Jo, she does not dismiss the idea of marrying for money, readers may misunderstand Amy. Amy is not more selfish than Jo, she is more canny. By this point in part two, Amy has already demonstrated the value of reason, understanding, thoughtfulness, getting along. If we return to the spot in part one where Marmee tells Meg and Jo what she wants for her daughters, the first descriptive word out of her mouth is "beautiful." It is Amy who has done what her mother wanted, who has used her looks, i.e., become beautiful in the eyes of society, to get ahead, but she has done so not out of vanity or greed but because, through her art, she has sought to understand the nature of beauty—in herself, in admiring Aunt March's jewelry, in painting, in relationships.

Once she departs on her trip, even though Amy is accompanied by her aunt, her uncle, and her cousin Flo (who seems to be about the same age), Amy is on her own in a way she has never been before—even on the ship, she is healthy and active, exploring the decks and the views, while "Aunt and Flo were poorly all the way." In the first letter she sends home, she remarks, "[G]entlemen really are very necessary aboard ship, to hold on to, or to wait upon one; and as they have nothing to do, it's a mercy to make them useful, otherwise they would smoke themselves to death, I'm afraid." Amy's trip is a whirlwind tour of what it means to be worldly, and she makes use of the opportunity. In general, her letters are amusing and high-spirited. She becomes involved in a practice romance, with one of Laurie's English friends, Fred Vaughn, but she understands that although Fred is strongly attracted to her, he is "rash," while she is "prudent" (well aware of all the lessons she has learned).

In the meantime, Jo gets away, too, though not as far

as Europe. Alcott's principal task for the rest of part two is to marry off Jo and Amy, and to do so in a way that her readers will accept, and that illustrates her theories about love, marriage, and money. I remember when I was reading *Little Women* as a girl, I sensed as soon as he entered that Professor Bhaer was to claim Jo, and I was put off—he was too old, too exotic. When I read it as an adult, I understand his appeal to Jo—he is witty and good-natured, easygoing, apparently able to calm her and advise her. Laurie, the handsome, youthful, energetic, talented, wayward young man, charges Jo up and triggers her pleasure in conflict, as is evident in the chapter "Heartache" when he proposes to her, over her own objections, and is argumentatively rejected. We all knew this was coming, but it is a sign of his passion that even though he knew it, too, he's willing to try. After she turns Laurie down, it is not implausible that Mr. Laurence might take him to Europe to forget Jo—Mr. Laurence has been the example of a wealthy American cosmopolitan all along. The difficult task is to get Amy and Laurie together in a believable and sympathetic manner, and Alcott begins by portraying the freshly minted grown-up Amy that Laurie encounters in Nice:

> As she stood at the distant window with her
> head half turned, and one hand gathering up her
> dress, the slender, white figure against the red
> curtains was as effective as a well-placed statue.

Amy is not attempting to woo Laurie—she is attempting
to show him that the girl he thought he knew is now a
woman who both fits in in Europe and does not—she
continues to possess certain American traits, such as a
love of physical activity, which she shows when they go
to a ball, and she "neither romped nor sauntered, but
danced with spirit and grace, making the delightsome
pastime what it should be." She doesn't dance with him
at first, but does something more effective: lets him
watch her and gauge her qualities from a distance as
she dances with other men. Then she sits with him and
demonstrates her new self-knowledge when they have
a straightforward and amusing conversation. In other
words, they are made for each other—they both can
operate skillfully in society and still manage to enjoy
themselves in the presence of others (because unlike
Jo, Amy minds her manners), but they can also have an
honest connection in which Amy, unlike many women

of her era, can speak and be heard, not in spite of her poverty, but because she has learned how to make the most of that very poverty. Laurie then monopolizes her for the rest of the evening.

Alcott is clear that Amy has not set her cap for Laurie, nor is she attempting to entrap him. After an interlude with Meg and John, we go back to Nice and observe how their relationship develops. They spend a lot of time together, and the more time they spend, the more Laurie is impressed, but Amy is not—she comes to have the same opinion of him that Jo and his grandfather have, that he is idling his youth away, has no purpose in life, always takes the easy way out. They go for a ride and then a walk, and she does again what she tried to do with Jo—to use reasoned argument to convince him to do what he should: to visit his grandfather, and thereby meet his obligations. She makes use of her talent for conversation and banter (even telling him "I despise you") to keep Laurie talking until he hears her true opinion, "Because with every chance for being good, useful and happy, you are faulty, lazy and miserable." He knows, having observed her for a month, that Amy herself is the example of someone who has chosen to make use of her chances to be good, useful, and happy, that she has put up with him and not pushed him away, as Jo did, and her "calm, cool voice" is more convincing than the frustrated appeals of others who have tried to reform him. And patience isn't her only weapon. Some time later, he looks at a sketch she has made of him lying in the grass. He sees his own idleness, but he also sees her artistic skill, and admires the way that her hard work has borne fruit. When he goes off to make use of his time and opportunities, she says she is glad he is gone, but she knows, maybe not as well as the reader knows, that she "shall miss him." Her attempt to argue Jo into reforming did not work, but her attempt with Laurie does.

After Beth's death, the question is not whether Amy and Laurie will marry—the reader already expects them to—but how they will get there, and so Alcott delves into their inner lives as they go about their business. Amy turns down Fred Vaughn, not angrily, but decidedly; Laurie tries pursuing art and music; when he composes an opera he wants Jo to be the female lead, but he can't put her in—she is too unappealing. He puts *someone* in, and that someone turns out, he realizes, to be based on his thoughts and feelings about Amy. She sends him pleasant letters and sketches and vows to be agreeable. Because they are traveling, the letters about Beth's illness never reach them, and when they separately get the news of her death, they rush to console each other. When Amy reunites with Laurie, she sees both their shared grief and his kindness, generosity, and love in coming from Germany to Switzerland to comfort her (and himself). In this way, Alcott defines their love as specifically theirs, made up of their psychological quirks and predispositions (let's say "nature" and "nurture," or "temperament" and "history"), and a contrast to the love Meg and John share, and the love Jo and Professor Bhaer share.

Jo accepts Professor Bhaer (they later go on to establish a progressive school rather like the schools that Alcott's father, Bronson, was known for). Jo must evolve, too, and she does, especially after she meets Professor Bhaer and understands that he offers her an opportunity that she never thought she would have: love. Laurie and Jo realize they are better as friends and brother and sister than they might have been as husband and wife—another definition of love—and Amy accepts that she might not have realized all her artistic ambitions, but she loves her life, her husband, and her frail baby daughter named after Beth—"the dread of losing her was the shadow over Amy's sunshine." Self-aware to the end, Amy tells her mother what she has learned. She says, "I never ought to [despair], while I have you to cheer me up, Marmee, and Laurie to take more than half of every burden . . . in spite of my one cross, I can say with Meg, 'Thank God, I'm a happy woman.'" Yes, Amy is the one to get the classic happy ending—true love, ideal mate, plenty of money, happiness, but from the beginning to the end of *Little Women*, Alcott has made sure that the reader knows that such an ending was earned through constant self-awareness and observation.

And here is the poignant postscript—May Alcott did make her name in the art world—a painting of hers, *La Négresse*, was exhibited at the 1879 Paris Salon, the most prestigious show in France, or, some say, in the world, at the time. Her painting was the only one by an American woman artist in the exhibition. And she did have a daughter, Lulu, whom she gave birth to at the age of thirty-nine. But May died when the baby was seven weeks old, and for the next eight years, Louisa raised Lulu until she herself died at the age of fifty-four.

The enduring appeal of *Little Women* ensures that readers will continue to contemplate the sisters, thinking and speaking of them as if they were real neighbors, friends, sisters—daughters. If Amy were my child, I would be proud of her—that she worked hard and sorted herself out in a methodical and productive way—and pleased with her, because she understands that pleasing others while adhering to her own goals is a good way to make peace in the family and, more generally, to maneuver through life. There are many women characters in novels (and women in life) who are thoughtful, cautious, observant, intelligent, and ambitious. Quite often, the words used to describe them are "cold," "calculating," "money-hungry," "shallow," "social-climbing." I consider these terms unfair and sexist. The artistic and political task that Alcott knows she must complete with Amy, and that she accomplishes, is integrating Amy's inner life and her actions so that the reader sees the complexity and subtleties of how she starts out and how she has fashioned herself. In some ways, this is more of a challenge than portraying the characters of Meg, Jo, and Beth, and it is evident as part two progresses and Alcott gives more time to Amy, especially to her self-expression, that she enjoys the challenge. Amy's emergence as a sensitive, thinking adult is one of the novel's more remarkable accomplishments. Amy is the modern woman, the thoughtful feminist; the sister who stays true to herself, learns to navigate her social world, gains a wisdom and self-knowledge different from that of her sisters, and is more like what we aim to be today.

ABOUT THE AUTHORS

KATE BOLICK's first book, *Spinster: Making a Life of One's Own*, is a distant descendant of Louisa May Alcott's writings about the single life. She lives in Brooklyn and teaches writing at New York University, but her heart remains in her hometown of Newburyport, Massachusetts, not far from where *Little Women* was born.

JENNY ZHANG is the author of the story collection *Sour Heart* and the poetry collection *Dear Jenny, We Are All Find*. She is the recipient of the Pen/Bingham Award for Debut Fiction and the Los Angeles Times Art Seidenbaum Award for First Fiction.

CARMEN MARIA MACHADO is the author of the story collection *Her Body and Other Parties*, which was a finalist for the National Book Award, and the forthcoming memoir *In the Dream House*. She'd like to thank Susan

Bailey—independent scholar and webmaster of Louisa May Alcott is My Passion—for generously sharing her transcriptions of Lizzie Alcott's surviving letters, and Will Gregg at Harvard University's Houghton Library for his assistance. She still thinks Jo should have let Amy drown.

JANE SMILEY has written many books for adults and children. Her most famous, *A Thousand Acres*, is not her favorite, but she learned a lot from writing it. Her favorites are lighter in tone—*Horse Heaven*, *Moo*, and her current kids' horse series. The second volume, about a contrary nine-year-old, was published in the spring of 2019. She is working on a nonfiction book titled *Five Mothers*, about her great-grandmother, her grandmother, her mother, herself, and her daughter. It will be published once all her relatives stop coming up with new information.

*The text in this book is set in 11 point Dante,
a face originally designed by Giovanni Mardersteig after
World War II and based on his experiences with the popular
book fonts Bembo and Centaur. The font acquired its name from
the first book in which it was used, Boccaccio's* Trattatello in
Laude di Dante. *It was redrawn as a digital font for Monotype
by Ron Carpenter in 1993. The sans serif font used for the running
heads is Gotham, designed by American type designer Tobias
Frere-Jones in 2000; for the chapter headings, Palomino Sans,
designed by British designer Elena Genova in 2018.*

*The paper is an acid-free, 60-pound Glatfelter stock with
an eggshell finish; it exceeds the requirements for permanence
of the American National Standards Institute. The binding
material is Arrestox, a cotton-based cloth with an aqueous
acrylic coating manufactured by Holliston, Church Hill,
Tennessee. Text design and composition by Gopa & Ted2, Inc.,
Albuquerque, New Mexico. Printing and binding by
Thomson-Shore Inc., Dexter, Michigan,*